# Waking Up Human

# Waking Up Human

## A SURVIVOR'S GUIDE

Susan Aranda

DRAKE STREET
PRESS

**Waking Up Human: A Survivor's Guide**
Published by Drake Street Press
Jacksonville, FL

Library of Congress Control Number: 2017958077

ISBN: 978-0-692-96954-0

SELF-HELP / Personal growth / Self-esteem

QUANTITY PURCHASES: Schools, companies, professional groups, clubs, and other organizations may qualify for special terms when ordering quantities of this title. For information, email WakingUpHuman.Life@gmail.com.

This book is printed in the United States of America

To Nella Mae Greene Sutton, my hero and guiding light,
who gave me her gift of words.


To my children, Camille and Clayton,
who each saved me in their own way by showing me
what real true love is and whom I would die to protect.

# Acknowledgments

To Polly Letofsky and her team at My Word Publishing.
To my editor, Bobby Haas, for dragging me out of my own shadows.

To all my abusers, for the lessons learned, and the battle scars that remind me every day just how hard I fought to maintain my beautiful, loving soul, the strength I carry within myself, and my certain knowing that love is always the answer.

To survivors and those seeking a way out: know you are not alone. You deserve to be loved, protected, and happy. Believe in yourself and the strength you possess inside to overcome and flourish. *Never give up.*

"He that hath an ear, let him hear what Spirit saith
unto the churches; To him that overcometh will I
give to eat of the tree of life, which is in the
midst of the paradise of God."
Revelation 2:7 (King James Version)


"Do not let your fire go out, spark by irreplaceable spark, in the
hopeless swamps of the approximate,
the not-quite, the not-yet, the not-at-all. Do not let
the hero in your soul perish, in lonely frustration for the life
you deserved, but have never been able to reach. Check your
road and the nature of your battle.
The world you desired can be won, it exists,
it is real, it is possible, it's yours."
Ayn Rand, *Atlas Shrugged*


"This above all—to thine own self be true, and it must follow,
as the night the day, thou canst not then be false to any man."
William Shakespeare, *Hamlet*

## Awakener

I am the awakener of songbirds,
carrying my message to humans
whose souls long for freedom.
Sing, child, sing!
Sing and share your story!
It will free you and
free those who need to hear it.
Your gift is your truth.
Those who would condemn be damned.
For they are afraid of owning their own.
They shall not pigeonhole
you into their oblivion.
Reject their stigma,
for they know you not
and have no right.

## Day 19,583

Damn. Again. I can never believe it, that first split second of waking up *human* in the morning. And don't even get me started on this morning thing. A totally irrational never-ending pain in the ass. Every morning is like being ripped from the womb all over again every single time. Human. Still. FUCK. I know with the utmost certainty that I was somewhere and something else before being human. I should have the hang of this by now. But I don't. Can't? Won't? Shall never? I am still figuring out my mission and purpose, but based on thorough research of past events from *this* life, it seems to be mainly about recovering myself from long periods of abuse by practically every human with some major relevance in my story, especially the ones who were supposed to be in charge of my care and nurturing up to and during adulthood. The other part of my mission and purpose, I have now realized, is to share my story, and all its darkness, in hopes of helping others reclaim their own light.

I have kept most of this abuse deep inside. It is painful to relive. Looking back, it is as if it happened to someone else until the memories stir up the emotions I felt during each incident. As I write this, I am picturing the opening scene from the movie *Romancing the Stone*, when Kathleen Turner's character, a romance novel writer, is crying and writing and crying and writing, disheveled and blotchy, as telling the story takes sacred precedence.

I was always told I am "just too sensitive," which made me feel even more alienated from the rest of the human population. I didn't *try* to feel things more deeply, see things more vividly, be sensitive to bright lights and loud sounds, or taste things so strongly (good and bad). I wasn't walking around waiting to get my feelings hurt. It's not like it was my fault. I was just living. Other people seemed like bulls in china shops to me, not just physically, but in their careless interactions with each other. I am just learning, in my fifties, that I am a highly sensitive person, or HSP. This means, according to some schools of thought, that I possess a high level of sensitivity to external stimuli and my central nervous system processes sensory data in a deeper, more thoughtful way. I am also extremely empathic; I feel other people's physical and emotional *stuff*. Most everyone is born with these gifts. Very few of us are born to human parents who are aware of and can teach us how to live with them. *Human lesson: is there a fix for this? Or was picking my way through treacherous territory one of the lessons I signed up for?*

Day 19,583 finds me a year and a half into taking care of my dad, who has end-stage Parkinson's disease and is on dialysis. One would be enough. Both together is like walking a tightrope and I wonder what the hell he is clinging to. He knows without a doubt that neither condition is curable. His quality of life is very low, at least from my perspective. But, I guess, who am I to question? I still don't understand all this.

I could write a separate book about caring for an elderly parent. To all former, current, and potential caregivers of aging and ailing parents: you are indeed very special souls. This is, without a doubt, one of the more exhausting parts of my journey. No one who hasn't done it themselves will ever fully understand. Prepare to be abandoned by other family members; it happens quite frequently. You will also become very isolated, as this duty takes priority over everything else in your life. Watching your parent wither away will be unbearable. It is going to get messy: emotionally, psychologically, and physically. Finding a support group is vital. But you got this.

I am a single mother. My daughter is nineteen and my son is thirteen. I remember them both as babies, but the growing-up part from then till now is kind of a blur due to their respective fathers dragging me through emotional hell. The climb out was strictly of my own volition and valiantly earned. Right now, the entire concept of mothering is foreign and feels like one hell of an imposition. Same for caregiving for the parent who never took care of me. Some days, I feel this way about my cats, too, and they never asked to be here, either.

Once upon a time, a long time ago, when I thought being human was finally a little bit ok, all I wanted was to love a man who loved me back and have a couple of babies and be the best wife and mother in the whole wide world. Probably just to prove to myself that it is supposed to be that way, and not the way my mother did it. So, ok, I got my babies.

I can't remember the girl who felt that way about everything. On day nineteen thousand five hundred eighty-three, I don't really even want to be here anymore. What if I want to change my mission in the middle of my mission? Is that possible? Because I am not sure I really like this one. *Being human is ~~hard~~ ~~difficult~~ ~~excruciating~~ bewildering.*

# Day 19,057

My father's wife passed one week ago today. She had stage four metastatic breast cancer, her third or fourth battle with cancer in ten years. Although her passing wasn't unexpected, it was sooner than we thought. I had plans with her that morning to help clean out their house. She had decided, three months prior, to move them to an apartment, a decision that stunned us all. Forty years of possessions to sort through, all while fighting cancer and taking care of a husband in stage two of Parkinson's disease with kidney failure imminent.

She didn't respond to my text that morning. When I called, her cell went straight to voicemail. She had mentioned not feeling well the night before. When I called the house phone, my dad answered and said he had heard her leave about 6:00 a.m. He even went to her room and didn't see her. I called her daughter who said she may have driven herself to the emergency room and she would check on her. Forty-five minutes later, I got the phone call that I knew was going to change my life. Dad packed a suitcase and came home with me that afternoon until we could have a family meeting and figure things out.

Yesterday, all the siblings met at the apartment to figure out what to do. I was concerned about what to do with Dad. He insisted he could take care of himself, but I knew that was not possible. Everyone else was digging through files and laptops looking for passwords and bank accounts. No one wanted to discuss Dad. Time's a-wasting, sisters. Let's talk. What are we going to do about Dad? There was complete silence. I could feel the reluctance hanging over the room. No one stepped up with any suggestions or offers.

So, I won/lost by default. Me. The single mother with two kids, two cats, and a demanding job. Not the sister who is married with grown children who don't live at home, not the single self-employed sister with an extra bedroom, and understandably not the single sister who lived out-of-state. Me. They would remind me later that *I chose* this; they think that absolves them of any guilt they feel.

This morning, I am exhausted, angry, overwhelmed, resentful, and bitter. On Day One after "the decision," Dad is on the couch with the fucking TV blaring unsettling, gory crime shows. I am trying to clean out the pantry, the fridge, the freezer, the kitchen cabinets, the guest bath, and every other space that has been turned upside down to accommodate a disabled elderly person. Everyone else is going about their happy little lives while mine is in complete chaos. I already want to run away from home.

# Day 8,798

While I was planning my first wedding, my parents were getting divorced. I had blissfully moved into my first apartment, finally away from the horror of my mother's abuse, but only after she Cinderella'ed me hard. I was working full-time and was responsible for cleaning up after everyone else and starting supper every afternoon when I got home. Then she decided I should do laundry for all six people on Saturdays. When she asked for rent on top of that, I finally got up the nerve to flee. So, I thank her for that. The apartment was one of the best times of my life. Solitude and the lack of daily wounding helped me begin to see some light in my life.

One day, the whole family came to help with something at my apartment. My dad drove separately and when everyone was ready to leave, he told them to go ahead, he was going to help me with something else. I hadn't asked him for any help, but I played along. After everyone left, this man, who provided for my physical needs quite well but never supported or nurtured me emotionally, and who knowingly left me in the clutches of the dragon, sat down on my couch and started to *cry real tears.* Jesus, are you kidding me right now? The only other time I saw him cry was at his father's funeral.

He proceeded to tell me that he had met someone. He had been seeing her for almost three years and she made him very happy. He was in love. She had given him an ultimatum: leave your wife or I am leaving you. I couldn't believe the man who had never given me any guidance was coming to *me* about this. Was he asking for my permission? Or was I the only soul who knew that the life he had lived with my mother justified the explosion that would follow his choice to end the marriage?

I also couldn't believe he was having any trouble making the decision. He lived in hell for 24 years. I asked him what he was waiting for. He felt his obligation to our family dictated waiting until my youngest sister graduated high school, a mere three months away. Hmmm, *obligation,* that's a telling choice of words, isn't it? On one hand, it sounds very noble of someone to suffer through torment to do what is "right." On the other, it would have been fulfilling to hear him say he was worried about the emotional toll this might take on his children. I told him he should just go; he looked like a man who might soon have a stroke. Oh, and by the way, the woman is also named Susan. Triple mind-fuck day. "Awkward" does not even begin to cover it.

My mother carried on like her hair was on fire. She just couldn't imagine why he would leave her after 24 years. It was interesting to watch her spin. I knew every move she was going to make and every word she was going to speak. At that time, I was not yet capable of giving truthful answers to her rhetorical questions. I was still afraid of being flayed alive. So I just watched it all unfold and tried to distance myself as often as possible. Who do you suppose became her emotional caretaker? That's right: the daughter she despised and mistreated. Good ol' me.

Until the day she said, "If your father is walking you down the aisle, I'm not coming to your wedding." I couldn't believe the words that came out of my mouth. "Ok, I'll send you pictures." And I totally meant it. Oh, hell, no, you are not taking *my* wedding down in flames because the man you victimized for your entire marriage finally had the courage to walk away.

The wedding went off without a hitch and she was coldly civil to my dad and his new girlfriend. She behaved herself with me for a very short period of time.

I was glad that my father found someone who seemed to make him happy. I supported his decision and his right to have a beautiful life. I even went to their wedding. And then he sort of disappeared from my life again. I knew he was making a new family. He hadn't been all that involved in my life up to this point. I pictured a new relationship between the two of us that never materialized. He seemed to be very involved with and quite fatherly toward his stepchildren when I did see him. Another little ouch to my psyche. Why didn't I count?

# Day 19,160

One hundred and three days into caregiving, and I hate my life. I work more than 50 hours a week and come home every day to work until bedtime. Someone told me this isn't a big deal; I am doing all the same things I always do, just for one extra person. The person who said that to me should be sentenced to one week in my shoes. Seriously. Dad's medication routine alone is mind-numbing. It takes me almost an hour every week to fill the pill boxes. At least I got some of his meds discontinued after speaking with his cardiologist and his neurologist. He is sleeping less and talking more. But, oh, the talking…

It seems he is only interested in one thing: sex. He has said the most inappropriate things a father could ever say to his daughter. Thankfully, they were not directed towards me, but I didn't need to hear his sexual opinions, preferences, and experiences. I am told this is the beginning sign of dementia, which sometimes occurs with Parkinson's. I have reminded him constantly that I am not his buddy, but it doesn't stop him.

His wife passed a little over three months ago and he is currently on a cruise with a former girlfriend. Thank God/dess I was not the one who had to take him to the doctor for erectile dysfunction pills or the drugstore for other supplies. I don't know how the hell he thinks he is going to have sex, since he can't even hold himself up. I mean, really, you have two degenerative, progressive, terminal diseases, and all you're worried about is your sex life? At least I am getting a four-day break in the action.

# Day 19,163

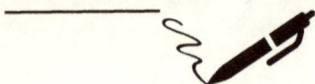

Cell phones and PWPs (persons with Parkinson's) do not mix. Today at work, my sister texted me that Dad kept calling her cell phone. Ok, did you call him to find out why? No, she did not. I called him to find out why he was calling her. Because the toilet is stopped up. OH MY GOD, you are a grown man and there is a plunger right next to the GDF'ing toilet. I cannot do anything about this from work, for fuck's sake. On my drive home, my cellphone rang as I was attempting to de-stress from the day by singing along with the radio at the top of my lungs. It was 5Star, the emergency service provided by Dad's cell carrier. He pushed the button and they can't reach him. Dear sweet baby Jesus, my head is going to explode.

## Day 19,168

Deactivated 5Star today after Dad called them no less than six times yesterday. *Human lesson: Whenever possible, remove the things from your life that tend to make your head explode.*

## Day 19,220

The past month has been like living in a war zone for me. Dad's kidney doctor says peritoneal dialysis is best for him. This involves an abdominal catheter, in other words, a *tube* sticking out of his body and equipment at home that will remove, clean, and replace abdominal fluid instead of doing conventional hemodialysis (blood) at a center. The process could be done several times during the day or continuously at night while he was asleep (um, he *doesn't* sleep and I can only imagine hooking and unhooking this equipment up several times per night). But wait: he can't do any of this himself. It will require steadiness and the use of both hands and an understanding of technology. His entire left side is stiff and weak from Parkinson's, especially his left hand. How am I going to work, take care of my kids, maintain a household, and be responsible for this? The surgery for the catheter has already been completed. Did anyone ask me about this?

No.

Post-surgery was a nightmare, too. Dad could not get off the couch or out of bed by himself for days. I got him a call button that rings a pager so I can at least go about my day without having to sit next to him. No bowel movement, either, so he's chugging the laxative.

And, also, he demanded that his six-foot-by-three-foot oak desk be brought here. Ok, do you plan to SLEEP ON TOP OF IT? Because there is nowhere else in this house it will fit. Guess what? I have rearranged my entire fucking bedroom to accommodate that stupid desk, adding insult to injury, in my opinion. Christ, I have rearranged this entire household and *my whole fucking life* to take care of him. How dare he?

And, also, the television. He will not watch anything but what *he* wants to watch. He has a TV and a recliner in his room. Selfish asshole! I do not have a TV in my room and I am sick to freaking death of your gory murder shows. I like music on, especially when I am in the kitchen. But, by all means, let's listen, at ear-bleed volume level, to every horrifying detail of how someone ended someone else's life.

The hell with peritoneal dialysis. I am going to have some semblance of a normal life. He can go to a dialysis center three times a week. I am done being treated like this by a self-centered jerk who deserted me my entire life. Fuck this shit.

He has fallen several times now while I was at work. Thankfully, he could get himself up. Also, he is forgetting to take his meds and sometimes not eating. I had to hire a caregiver for weekdays. I have to prepare his breakfast and lunch for the week so the caregiver can give him appropriate meals. This will be a whole new adventure, but hopefully I can focus on my job while I am at work.

# Day 19,238

Dad is on a trip with his siblings. I have eight glorious days off-duty. I hope they can handle him, because he cannot handle himself. We had a fun Friday night at the ER because his "breathing wasn't right." *Yes, I know, I have explained a million times that Parkinson's causes weakness in the muscles involved in swallowing and breathing, which is why the neurologist recommended physical therapy that you refused. There is nothing wrong with your breathing, but let's go hang out for hours and hours in the ER.* Bought him a wedge pillow so he can sleep in an elevated position. I'm told this will keep him from feeling like he can't breathe.

Parkinson's also causes dysphagia, difficulty swallowing, something that could have been delayed with physical therapy. Mealtime is horrific, as Dad chokes and coughs with every bite, all while continuing to cram food in his mouth. This means he is probably aspirating (inhaling food particles and liquids into his lungs). Aspiration pneumonia is the leading cause of death in Parkinson's patients. But he refuses to listen to me. Apathy, depression, and denial on his part are winning. I can't help him if he won't help himself.

He has fallen three times within four days. At 4:00 a.m., he fell backwards into the bathtub after standing up from the toilet. Blood everywhere. The EMTs came. His blood pressure was 100/60, even after that frightening episode. He refused to go to the hospital and almost fell again getting up from the couch to go back to bed. He fell the next morning at midnight. Another fall the next afternoon as the caregiver was bringing him home from an appointment. I bought him a walker, which he refuses to use.

He started taking Ambien two days before the falls started. My research revealed that Ambien significantly lowers blood pressure. Why on earth would a neurologist prescribe this for a Parkinson's patient? Parkinson's and the meds used to treat it can lower blood pressure, and Parkinson's patients have balance issues.

I called to ask if we could try another prescription for insomnia. The neurologist's response was that meds were doing all they could for Dad; it is time to look for a long-term care facility. Wrong answer, dude. First of all, my dad isn't a throwaway, regardless of how I feel about him. Secondly, how are you unaware that Medicare does not cover long-term care for Parkinson's disease? *Human lesson: Doctors do not always have the right answer. Do your own research.*

## Day 19,287

Chaos continues to reign, despite my best efforts. More surgery, this time to graft an artery to a vein (called a fistula) in preparation for upcoming hemodialysis. Because that needs to start sooner than later, they also put in something called a permacath, which is actually temporary—go figure. It is an opening directly to a blood vessel in his chest. The permacath's instructions are DO NOT SHOWER, do not get wet, and all sorts of other fun things to send me into a panic. I explained that if he messes with it, he could get an infection that will go into his bloodstream. He will not listen to me.

Then Dad was admitted to the hospital for a pulse under 50 beats per minute. Many tests, no cardiac issues. Determination: kidney failure. Two dialysis treatments in hospital and regular Monday, Wednesday, and Friday dialysis treatments began. Swallow study revealed silent aspiration. All liquids must be thickened to honey consistency. Oh, joy, something else to add to the routine. Discharged from hospital. Weak, distant, uncommunicative. He missed the chair sitting down to breakfast. Thankfully, I caught him before he hit the floor, but I couldn't get him up. We are now on a first-name basis with the EMTs. Dad hasn't been able to get off the couch unassisted since hospital stay (except when I am not looking and he wants a beer), but today he decided to walk two blocks down to the pond. *Could you have been considerate enough to ask me when I might have time to walk you down to the pond? I AM COOKING YOUR STUPID SPECIAL FOOD FOR THE WEEK and I am not stopping in the middle of what I am doing.* He went by himself. FINE, then.

Another fall into the tub getting up from the toilet after the caregiver left. I had stopped for groceries on my way home from work. Dad's medical alert pendant did not work, so he laid there for about an hour yelling for help. He had also helped himself to not one, but *two* laxative suppositories (those are no longer within his reach, thank you very much, live and learn), so there was blood and shit everywhere. I had to clean him up before I called rescue to help get him out of the tub and assess his injuries.

Yet another fall, this time backwards out of the tub when he finished his shower. I told him no more showers at night. The caregiver can help him shower before she leaves at 5:00 p.m. on non-dialysis days. His primary care physician already told him it is not good for his skin, which is like paper, to shower every day. He didn't listen. He got in the shower while I was doing something else. And fell. Again. I am furious. This seems selfish of him. I know he is trying to maintain his independence, but his foolish decisions are making it harder for me to take care of him.

I am totally fucking drained. *Human lesson: You cannot grant an elderly disabled person the luxury of independence if it means they run the risk of being injured. Tough love reigns here. Be the bad-ass authoritarian you have to be.*

# Day 19,292

Have I mentioned the shitfest that has become a constant daily occurrence? Parkinson's and its meds cause constipation. In fact, researchers now believe that chronic constipation is one of the earliest indicators of Parkinson's. My dad has always fought with digestive issues and constipation. Constipation causes hemorrhoids. My dad has those in spades. Hemorrhoids bleed quite often from constipation.

Laxatives do not always work with Parkinson's patients. There is a whole list of medical terms for it, but basically, muscle weakness and glitches in the autonomic nervous system (responsible for things like heart rate, breathing, and digestion) mean that no matter what you put in, nothing may come out—or at least not as quickly as one might hope.

After I removed the laxatives from Dad's reach, he found a new way to help the poop out. I became aware of this new trick one Saturday afternoon when I went to give him his lunch. He now eats all meals in his lift chair, which my sister helped locate and have delivered. It is blue, even though I begged her to get the green one that would *almost* fit in with my living room décor. *Please, just one little normal thing since my life is already a cluster-fuck.* But no, she picked the *blue* one. It sticks out like a big, blue, sore thumb, and I fucking hate it and her.

I put on his bib and brought his lunch over to his tray. I couldn't shake the smell of something not quite right. He was cramming food into his mouth. Then I saw his fingernails. They were caked with feces. Upon closer inspection, they were caked with *bloody feces.* You have got to be motherfucking kidding me.

I screamed at him to stop putting food in his mouth with shit on his hands, but had to wrestle the food away from him. As I ran to the bathroom to get sanitary wipes, I saw the trail…of…bloody…feces. FUCK MY LIFE. It was everywhere he could possibly have touched. The toilet seat, the toilet handle, the sink, the faucet, the towel, the bathroom doorknob, the handles of his walker. I asked him how this happened and he said the unthinkable: he dug the poop out with his fingers. I am hyperventilating at the horror of the germs that he spread everywhere, including into his own mouth. I felt my brain snap. I explained how dangerous this was, especially with bleeding hemorrhoids. I know he isn't listening. I ordered nitrile gloves and surgical masks. And a lot more disinfectant. I think my sisters should come over and play. In the shit. *Human lesson: Just when you think things can't get any worse, they will. Hope for the best, but try and anticipate the worst so you have a game plan.*

## Day 19,300

Being a good Southern girl (and, yes, if you are one, Southern is always capitalized), I know and value the healing power of certain foods. Take biscuits, for example. My Mimi made them best. Hers were not big fluffy biscuits; they were small and crispy on the outside and full of heaven on the inside. I can *almost* make them as good as she did. Though mine will never be quite the same, they have the whisper of Mimi in them.

# Mimi's Biscuits

2 cups sifted flour
4 t. baking powder
1/2 cup buttermilk
1/2 t. salt
¼ t. baking soda
2/3 cup shortening

Sift together flour and dry ingredients. Cut in shortening (with a fork if you don't have a pastry blender) until mixture resembles coarse crumbs. Add buttermilk all at once; stir only until dough follows fork around bowl. Turn out on lightly-floured surface. Knead GENTLY for 30 seconds; over-kneading tends to make the biscuits tough. Pat out to ½ inch thick. Cut with biscuit cutter. Bake on an ungreased cookie sheet in very hot oven (425°) for 10-12 minutes.

You can't have biscuits without gravy; white gravy, or milk gravy. My mother did make a pretty mean gravy. It was one of the first cooking skills I mastered. It's a tradition passed down through generations. Every family's gravy is just a wee bit different. Why is gravy so soul-satisfying? I do not know and I don't care to unravel the mystery. It might take something away, like Dorothy seeing behind the Wizard's curtain. I love gravy so much, I wrote it a poem. It goes like this:

## The Power of White Gravy

I mean true Southern milk gravy, of course.
The kind my Mimi always made.
Hell, I never knew such a thing as
brown gravy even existed
till I was a grown woman
(and I cannot abide it!).
Hot drippings from whatever meat was cooked
(Bacon gravy is my favorite).
Stir in the flour -
FAST
so it doesn't lump or burn.
When the time is right,
add the milk and –
STIR, STIR, STIR!
Watch it get thick,
add salt and pepper
(while your mouth waters),
and voila!
HEAVEN.
There's a fine art to the dance of making gravy.
I learned it well
but I don't practice it nearly enough.
White gravy makes everything better –
including
my soul.

I think I definitely need more gravy in my life, considering
everything that's going on.

# *Day 19,324*

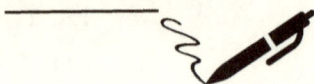

D ear God/dess, can this man please fucking *sleep*? The pager goes off at least twice a night for trips to the bathroom. There is no peeing. Dad is just awake. Sometimes he pages to just to see if I will respond. Those were his exact words. Occasionally, the Parkinson's Monkey in his brain will cause him to do this repeatedly throughout the night.

My alarm goes off at 5:30 a.m. on weekdays. I haven't had more than three consecutive hours of sleep in months. I am beginning to question my own sanity. Parkinson's also causes insomnia. We have tried everything. I could turn off the pager, but Mr. Hardheaded would just get out of bed by himself and fall. I am the walking dead living with the dying.

I am waiting on Dad hand and foot since he practically lives in the lift chair. And do you think he could utter a "please" or "thank you?" Not to me. He only plays nice with caregivers and nurses at doctors' offices. Is this a Parkinson's thing or is it his personality? It's like I am not even a human being. I don't expect constant gratitude, but a little respect for the daughter he threw away who is now devoting her life to taking care of him would be nice.

Yet another trip to the ER. Dad cut the end off the abdominal catheter that has yet to be removed since we won't be doing peritoneal dialysis after all. He says he doesn't know why he did it. Now he has an open tube sticking out of his body. Stuff can come out, but, more importantly, stuff can go in, like GERMS. He had to stay the night because they couldn't find a cap to fit the tube.

Oh, and when we got to the ER, there was shit caked under his fingernails. I handed my sister some wipes and said, "Your turn." The digging out of poo continues daily. I understand that it is miserable to be constipated. If he were self-aware enough to thoroughly clean up, I would say go for it. But he isn't and I am sick to death of literal shit. Here's my new Christmas carol: "Deck the halls with smears of feces, fa-la-la-la-la, la-la-la-la. Clean it up, don't go to piec-ies, fa-la-la-la-la, la-la-la-la." *Human lesson: Maintaining a sense of humor will keep you from going off the deep end.*

# Day 19,369

Another 911 call to get Dad up off the bathroom floor. Thankfully, no injuries this time. Two days later, my daughter calls as I am on my way to work. Dad is on the floor in his room, but up against the door, so no one can get in to help him. Why the hell didn't he stay in bed until the caregiver arrived? FINE, then. Call 911 and I am on my way home. By the time I got there, the EMTs had managed to get into his room. He hit his head on the dresser.

We talked him into going to the hospital for concussion evaluation, which was negative. This time, I let the paid caregiver stay with him. Fuck the overtime it will cost. Three days in the hospital due to extremely low blood pressure until the doctor realized Dad had a do-not-resuscitate order and sent him home. He fell in the bathroom the next day after the caregiver left. I do not understand why he cannot sit in his chair for the thirty minutes after she leaves and before I arrive home from work.

## Day 19,382

I am reclaiming part of my life. After almost a year of serious sleep deprivation, I have made the executive decision to hire a nighttime caregiver, Monday through Friday, 10:00 p.m. to 6:00 a.m. I need to sleep if I am going to keep my job and my sanity. I deserve this much.

I have tried my best to preserve Dad's assets, especially since we have no idea how long this could go on. But I will be damned if I am going to sacrifice my health for his. I have had little to no help from anyone. If it weren't for the caregivers' group I found on social media, I would have already lost my mind. Weekends suck hard as he can no longer get out of bed, dress, or feed himself. If nothing else, I am going to get a good night's sleep Monday through Friday.

# Day 19,409

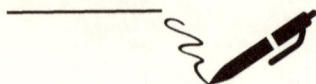

B ack to the damned hospital due to collapse of fistula. More surgery to place a temporary catheter for in-hospital dialysis until the fistula can be repaired. Seven days in the hospital this time. I had the nighttime caregiver spend the nights there with him so I could get some sleep and be at work. Every day in the hospital requires three days of recovery time after discharge. I know what's ahead: three weeks of weakness, listlessness, and not being able to get around without help.

I quit my job. My sister and brother-in-law suggested this. I had a horrible day at work the same day Dad ended up back in the hospital, which led me to have a complete breakdown. I want them to remember that this was their idea. Yes, my job was toxic, and it was good for me to leave.

However, what no one except me considered was that now, on top of approximately $10,000 per month in paid caregiver expenses, which is roughly twice the amount of his monthly pension (his existing expenses include the Medicare "gap" that requires him to pay through the nose for some prescriptions and the additional equipment and supplies he constantly needs), he would now be paying all my household expenses as well. And, yes, putting a monthly stipend in my bank account. That is very little to ask for someone who is on duty 24/7. I let the night person go and took over that shift of caregiving. Still no sleep at night, but no job means I can sleep during the day, like a vampire.

Let's consider my duties, by the way. It is *not* just like adding an extra person to the household. This person needs special consideration in every aspect of his life. He cannot manage his own finances. He cannot shop for his own groceries, which include a long list of special items due to his dietary restrictions. Heart disease, diabetes, kidney failure and Parkinson's all have their own requirements that sometimes conflict with one another. I am constantly schlepping to the grocery store for something that was consumed more often than the meal plan called for. I had to buy a second refrigerator for the garage to hold most of *our* food since there wasn't room in one refrigerator.

Dad cannot prepare his own meals. I spend most of every Sunday on meal prep just for *his* food. There is constant laundry thanks to incontinence and the mess from him insisting on feeding himself. His bathroom must be inspected and cleaned after every use due to the never-ending poo festival.

I have stopped trying to keep up with the stains on the carpet from his drooling, incontinence, and food accidents. There are scuff marks on the walls and doorways of his path because he can't push the walker straight. Also, this house was not exactly designed for the disabled. I will surely lose my security deposit and then some when I move. Did anyone think about that financial burden? Nope.

Now let's add managing the clusterfuckapalooza of caregivers. Some have been great; some have not. Even the great ones look to me for leadership. Every time one leaves, I am the trainer of the new person. And it has been a revolving door of caregivers. Some left on their own, some I let go. There is no stability here. As soon as I put out one fire, three more are instantly raging. No lie. I don't know how I managed to keep my job for as long as I did.

# Day 19,471

Just put Dad and his caregiver on a plane to Nashville. I have six glorious days off-duty. It is about fucking time. I am super weary of hearing about other family members' church obligations, dinner reservations, music festivals, and weekend trips. I get that they are probably as emotionally detached from Dad as am I, but I thought they might give a crap about *me*. Dad is not quite as portable as he was in the beginning, though, so it would just be too much for someone else to take him for a weekend. How about someone comes over here? I would happily take my kids to a hotel somewhere fun!

In the past two months, there has been yet another hospital stay (damned fistula), another confirmed progression of Parkinson's, several more falls, and inappropriate commentary. This time it was about my boobs. I have tried to overlook him staring at them constantly, but when he started talking about them, I lost my shit. Listen, old man, FIRST OF ALL, I am your DAUGHTER; my boobs are off-limits. Secondly, nice to know that women are valued in your mind by the size of their mammary glands. Thirdly, perhaps if you had seen women as something other than boobs, you might have made better choices. My dad staring at my tits: Best. Memory. *Ever.* Thanks, Dad. *Human lesson: Nothing is as serious as it seems. Laugh, dammit.*

# Day 19,495

In order to preserve some level of sanity, I have declared that Dad must wear an adult diaper at night. The last two times we tried to go to the bathroom in the middle of the night, he was so unsteady that he almost took us both down. We tried a potty chair next to the bed, but that was a no-go also. He has no balance and turning around is a recipe for disaster. This means, you understand, that I must coat his bottom with diaper rash cream every night. Another breach of my boundaries. And his. I realize how narcissistic I must sound, but I am completely devoid of any but the most basic level of compassion at this point.

He can no longer be left alone to feed himself. He stuffs his mouth so full that food is falling out onto his bib as he is shoving more in. I have to watch him like a hawk. At times, he is unable to swallow food or medication. What happens next? I am afraid to ask.

## *Day 19,540*

Here's what happens next: Dad suddenly stopped chewing. Wondered why it was taking him over two hours to finish a meal, besides the obvious coughing and choking. He coughed up big chunks of unchewed food. He is swallowing bites of food whole. Dear fucking God. Now I am pureeing everything. Meat, vegetables, oatmeal and eggs, *every single freaking thing he eats* must now be the consistency of baby food. Talk about cooka-palooza. That's all I will be doing. But he will still choke. He's choking on yogurt.

Since I can't get anyone to take Dad for a weekend or even stay here with him regularly, I have hired a weekend nights care-giver. I deserve to get the hell out of Dad purgatory at scheduled intervals. I, too, would like to have dinner reservations and at-tend local events. I need some light in my life.

At his annual visit with his primary care physician, who diagnosed the Parkinson's disease, the doctor was shocked to see that he is down to 120 pounds, but said it is due to the Parkinson's and there is not much we can do. She also told him she didn't think he was going to make it to his next neurologist's appointment in two months. Parkinson's would take him first. She wrote orders for hospice palliative care, although we didn't tell him it was hospice. Here we go.

# Day 19,561

I have a whole new comprehension of the word "overcrowded." We now have an oxygen machine, a transport chair, a new shower chair, a new potty chair, and a whole new system of medication delivery and dispensation. More logs and charts to keep up with. And more people. Hospice sends an RN once a week, a bath person three times a week, a social worker once a month, and a chaplain as needed. I am happy for the help, and the hospice staff are all exceedingly wonderful, but my phone is constantly buzzing with people confirming appointments. Some days it is like a three-ring circus in my house. I still manage paid caregivers, dialysis, and the kidney doctor. All other doctors are off the case once palliative care began.

We've been to the outpatient center twice in the past month for fistula repair. No one can really explain to me why the fistula is constantly blocked, but at least they are able to correct it. Dialysis will continue until Dad decides to stop or Parkinson's ends his life. So, we must maintain access to the fistula.

New words Dad has used: "dick" and "pecker." Honestly, he used to be so modest. I have learned to throw it right back at him. It is commonly known I can swear like a sailor. This man actually said to me he didn't think I should use the word "motherfucker." I responded that in this case, it's appropriate, no? Also, in some cultures they say "sisterfucker." Would he like me to use that instead?

New tricks Dad can do: sliding out of the lift chair onto his butt on the floor. Why? I wish I knew. He pages me eighty-seven-bajillion times during the night, but refuses to page me if he is sitting in that damned lift chair. He tries to get up and go to the bathroom by himself. Oh, and did I mention the most currently annoying trick? He uses the remote to that lift chair non-stop, just riding the chair up and down, and up and down, like it's an amusement park ride. I wouldn't care, except I can *hear* the damned thing, and then I go on high alert. After three consecutive hours of that this weekend, I took the remote away and unplugged the chair. A girl's gotta have a break.

Oh, and also, he can no longer even use the walker by himself. Whoever is here, me included, has to hug him from behind when he's ambulating to A) keep him going straight and B) keep him from falling backwards. He has no balance left.

## Day 19,573

More of the same. My life is a shitstorm, literally. I live from mess to mess. This is like backwards potty-training. There are just as many urine-related accidents as poop festivals. I will *never* get used to this. Each incident is an assault on my senses and my soul. Where did my compassion go? Up in flames, like the rest of my life.

Weekend nights caregiver quit. Her replacement seems competent and caring. Wonder how long she will last? I fired the daytime caregiver, who has been the only constant in our lives. She was with us for almost eight months. Unfortunately, she became almost a member of the family and I needed a professional who could be objective. She did an amazing job, until she didn't. And she helped herself to my chicken salad and the love of my children. Um, nope.

# Day 19,579

Also known as "The Fishing Trip That Almost Didn't Happen," or Clusterfuckapalooza Volume II. I put out a call to action on social media to find someone with a boat who could accommodate Dad's lack of mobility and give him one last fishing trip. A wonderful friend of a friend generously offered to take us out on his boat for an afternoon. I was so excited for Dad! I shopped for boat gear and packed lunch for us both. I loaded up the car. Then I went inside to get him.

This is when it all went south in a big hurry. (By the way, why is "going south" a derogatory term? I LOVE the south! I AM the south.) The daytime caregiver had mentioned that Dad occasionally tried to open his car door or attempted to move the gear shift despite her cautions while they were driving to dialysis. Well, I found out exactly what she meant. He absolutely refused to listen to anything I said beginning the moment we were headed out the front door. I told him to stop long enough for me to lock the front door before I put him in the car. NOPE.

When we got to the boat ramp, I calmly explained that I was going to leave the car running with the air conditioning on and that he needed to stay put in his seat until I got everything out of the trunk. I hadn't even finished talking before he opened his door. I restated my instructions and the reasons behind them. I needed him to be still so he didn't fall in the parking lot and bust his head open. Please wait for me to help you out of the car. He didn't listen. I told him if he didn't do what I asked, we would just go back home. Still doing his own thing. By the time I finally was ready to get him out of the car, I was a screaming maniac.

The fishing trip went fine. There was no drama until we got home. The same disregard for instructions designed for his safety. Cognitive reasoning is out the window. Impulse control is gone. My brain is exploding.

# Day 19,584

But, let's talk about the cool things that are here for humans. Like tonight, there is a super-bright quarter moon, wispy clouds scudding by, lightning in the distance, and enough breeze to tinkle the wind chimes. Did I mention I really, really, really like wind chimes? They are like the voice of the wind singing a secret. I have a love-hate relationship with my garden. Pass/Fail kind of thing. Weeds make me want to scream, although I am told that weeding is therapeutic. I freaking hate it with all that I am. Once I create something, I want it to just BE and not need further maintenance. I have hummingbirds, bumble bees, agopastomen bees (they are a freaky shade of green!), butterflies, lizards, tree frogs, toads, and snails, to name a few of the creatures who come to hang out.

Other things I like are thunderstorms and beaches, mountains and valleys, rivers and streams. Oh, and COFFEE. Oh my gosh, how I love coffee. Is there coffee on The Otherside? I am told there is, so that isn't just a human experience. And music. Well, I have no words to describe the effect music has on me. But there is also music on The Otherside. There are good smells. There is delicious food. There is color and sound and smell and touch and sight. All of these exist elsewhere, so what is the point of being human? Did I choose this? If so, was I delirious at the time? Is there a bail-out clause in my contract somewhere? Where is my legal counsel?

## Day 19,585

Same. It's like the movie *Groundhog Day*, although the day's clusterfucks invariably vary. That makes things infinitesimally less monotonous, I suppose. FINE, then. This phrase sums it all up and became a personal meme when it first came out of my three-year-old daughter's mouth in response to finally grasping the concept that "no" means "no" and she was not going to be able to get her way. The ultimate phrase of indignant, defiant, but very much *temporary*, resignation.

## Day 19,587

———————

Honestly, what is this "human" thing, anyway? A body that seems to get in the way of my soul. I feel like I am driving a jalopy when I should be in a Cadillac. A black one. With very dark tinted windows. Really, the bizarrity—bizarre hilarity—of it all is enough to consume a human for a year or two just puzzling it through. So, how did I get here, to day nineteen thousand five hundred and eighty-seven? Let's review.

Birth: exactly 6:47 p.m. on a Monday night, December 31, 1962, in a place on Earth called Tennessee (which is very beautiful, I must say). Let's look at some of these clues about my entrance into the physical realm and why my soul chose this particular time to become human. I am not sure why I chose December. I am not a fan of cold weather. However, I am very much a Capricorn, the symbol for which is a sea-goat, half goat, half fish. Here's what Wikipedia has to say about my sign: The mountain goat part of the symbol depicts ambition, resoluteness, intelligence, curiosity, but also steadiness, and the *ability to thrive in inhospitable environments* while the fish represents passion, spirituality, intuition, and connection with the soul. Oh, indeed! Also, Capricorn is the third and last of the earth signs, one of the other two being Taurus. My dad is a Taurus. Monday is the moon's day, I've discovered. In Old English, *Mōnandæg*, in Middle English, *Monenday*, a translation of the Latin *dies lunae*, which means "day of the moon." No wonder I have always considered myself a moon child; I AM! Coincidentally (not), the year 1962 began and ended on a Monday.

The world was changing rapidly as I was preparing to enter human form. Was my mother affected by world events such as race riots, the Cuban Missile Crisis, the first man to orbit the earth, the emergence of The Beatles? Did she fear or hope for the future of the world, or was she absorbed, as is natural, by events closer to home?

Parents: angry, narcissistic mother; emotionally and sometimes physically unavailable father.

Siblings: three younger sisters; the four of us are 18 months apart all the way down the line.

Environment: utter depths of hell with plenty of absolute emotional chaos and turmoil thrown in for good measure. If you are unfamiliar with the concepts of parenting mentioned above, first of all, lucky you. Secondly, please Google them. It would take me another nineteen thousand, five hundred and eighty-seven days to fully explain the depth and breadth of the torment.

In this type of dynamic, there is always a scapegoat, usually the oldest child (ME), and a golden child, usually the youngest child. The middle children are lost in the shuffle, as long as they don't cause any trouble. The narcissist is good at the old "divide and conquer" maneuver. If my sisters and I all told about our relationship with our mother, you might think we were raised in different households. It is definitely not a cohesive family unit. My mom made me responsible for my sisters' behavior and punished me whenever they did something wrong. They were allowed to lie about me in order to get me in trouble. In short, there was a great deal of emotional and psychological trauma that resulted in negative self-esteem and thoughts of suicide.

Oh, yeah. Suicide. I wanted to talk about that. That's a game-changer, right? I, for one, obviously, as previously mentioned, can tell you how someone gets to the point of considering suicide. I can tell you why they think, hope, dream of it. I can explain the perspective of someone who is drowning in the emotional and psychological torrent for which there appears to be absolutely no dry land nor end in sight. When a person first lets their brain give even a passing nod to the subject of suicide, they feel completely helpless, powerless, or just too damned worn out to change their circumstances. They've been fighting too long. There is no hope left. "I can't take this anymore and I know I can't stop whatever is causing the pain." NO HOPE. It is not about punishing those left behind. It is about putting an end to the unbelievable pain, emptiness, and complete and utter despair.

I am no longer suicidal. I was granted the grace of having the strength to endure "just a little longer," in case things did get better because deep down inside I truly believed they were supposed to. I never attempted suicide. I can't speak for anyone who has. I am one of those "don't like to leave before the end of the movie" people, even if the movie sucks hard. I guess those two things are what kept me from following through, and once I became a mother, suicide never entered my mind.

# Day 1,066

The abuse began when I was around three, so sometime before I had been human for one thousand days. The second daughter would have been 18 months old and the third daughter due any day. I loved my baby sisters. I have always loved babies. Babies are love. Babies do not yell at you. They just look at you with a holiness and adoration pouring out of their eyes.

I do not remember the first thing, or the second, or the third. I don't remember the exact words that were said. I do recall suddenly being aware one day that my mother had changed and the demon who took her place absolutely despised me and lived to torment me. I was a nervous wreck, as the attacks were always sudden and not prompted by anything I did or didn't do—at least not that I could ever figure out. This is when I began chewing my fingernails down to the quick and became riddled with such overwhelming anxiety that my stomach was constantly in knots. I have been *on guard,* on high alert ever since; to date, 51 years.

This also set up the self-doubt and self-loathing that followed me into my late 40s and brought with it a stunning number of other abusive relationships, and a great many physical ailments. I abruptly went from always being a good girl to the most vile and worthless piece of garbage ever to have been born. Deeper still was the idea planted into my brain that I was intrinsically wrong; as in, God didn't make you right on purpose, you don't deserve it. You are flawed to the core and even God doesn't like you. This was reinforced by good ol' religion when I transitioned from Sunday school, where we learned the "Jesus Loves Me" song, to "big church," where the first sermon I heard told me I was born a sinner and there was nothing I could do to change that. I could only pray to God to save me.

When God doesn't answer your prayers, you begin to believe this is true and, paradoxically, doubt the existence of God. When you're three, and the mother-thing hates you, who do you think is the "bad" one? You believe you are, of course. Mother-things don't lie, right? This is what I call "the great mindfuck." I learned it well and practiced it on myself a great many times in my life.

I remember very vividly one time staring out the plate-glass window in the living room and screaming inside my head for my real mother to come back, that a witch had taken her place and no one knew it but me; she had even fooled the daddy. *She suddenly became someone else.* So there must have been good times, if not emotional bonding, before the abuse started. Aha, perhaps this is why I immediately assume I've committed some unconscious error when a new friend doesn't behave the same way I would. I am always waiting for *someone to become someone else.*

Abandonment is the sub-program always running in the background of my mind.

I also remember that the verbal abuse became such that I would be in the fetal position with my hands over my ears trying to block out further assaults. Because I am a very sensitive and empathic soul, not only did the words feel like physical blows, I could also feel her rage and hatred. The attacks became physical whenever I resisted listening to the verbal assaults, and also as the years and abuse progressed. It was almost always sudden and unpredictable; I would be playing or watching TV and the next thing I knew I was being hit and she was screaming at me and I would be trying to protect myself from the blows and I would be screaming back at her "I'm sorry, Mommy! I'm sorry, Mommy! What did I do?"

Early on, after a cooling-off period, came apologies and hugs and kisses and tears from her. I always believed her. Until the time the thought of her hugging me physically repulsed me. I was maybe four, so I didn't have the awareness of understanding why I didn't want her to hug me. She was *furious,* which led to more verbal abuse. That's the day I realized, without knowing what it was, that she was a liar about ever being sorry for what she consistently did to me.

One day, she must have lost track of the time, because she was in my room reducing me to a sobbing mass with her words and my father came home from work. This was one of the few times he ever confronted her about the abuse. He said something to the effect of how dare she, I was only a child, and he'd better not ever catch her doing that again. She made damned good and sure he never *caught* her again, at least until it had gone on long enough that he no longer protested. The first abandonment: the mother *who suddenly became someone else.* The second abandonment came soon after when my mother began to abuse me in front of my father, who turned a blind eye.

My grandmother was my only lifeline. I was four or five before I couldn't keep it to myself anymore and ran sobbing to her arms one day when we went to see her. I was trying very hard not to cry, but I could feel the dam break as she asked me what was wrong. I could barely choke out the words "Mommy hates me" before the sobbing started. Mimi assured me I was wrong. I told her that she had said so to me, almost every day…at about that time, my mother walked in with derisiveness dripping from her tongue. There was a very brief but adamant admonition to my mother by my Mimi. Of course, she could not stop the demon. I cried myself to sleep in her arms as only a child can. The first release. But, boy, did I ever pay for that sweet moment.

I was completely ALONE. No one to nurture or guide me, just someone to avoid at all costs, which was, naturally, impossible. Nursery school and kindergarten came along and my teachers always praised me for being good. Their praise made me feel like a fraud and I was determined that they must not ever find out the truth about me—the things only my mother knew about me and how horrible I really was. I lived in dark despair and complete terror. And yet somehow, deep inside, I knew that it wasn't supposed to be like this.

When I was five, I got the unimaginable news that we were moving to another city three hours away. At the time, I thought the mother-thing had done this on purpose. Years later, I finally understood it really was because of my dad's job. My second thought was "OH NO, NO MIMI." I would have no access to the only person in my life who showed me any love and who knew the truth of what my mother was doing to me. I died inside. I was a child, less than six years of age, in complete and utter mourning. I couldn't see the sunshine to save my life. I cared about absolutely nothing. But on the day we moved into our new house, a miracle happened: God gave me my Kevin. *Human lesson: There will always be a silver lining.*

# Day 19,589

It's a Thursday. This day of the week thing is kind of strange, too. Wonder when it went from seven days a week of doing your own thing to working five days for someone else and having only two days to be you? I have so many ideas about how this could be better. It would require a community of people with honesty and integrity, though, and that seems to be in short supply among the human population in the Year of Our Lord two-thousand and sixteen. Oh, sure, modern conveniences spurred by the Industrial Revolution are astonishing and (mostly) pleasant, but a very large part of me longs to be living on a plot of land somewhere growing my own food and tending my chickens. I've never done either of these things, but the notion appeals to me greatly. Now that women are no longer Suzy Homemakers, I feel nostalgic for something that never happened for me. I am certain a conversation with former June Cleaver types might change my mind, but we always seem to want what we don't have.

I don't currently look forward to weekends. After I quit my full-time job to manage Dad's care, the schedule was for a caregiver from 8:00 a.m. to 4:00 p.m. Monday through Friday and on Friday and Saturday evenings from 4:00 p.m. to midnight. That means SaturDAY and Sunday, I have him all by myself. The weekends get pretty dark around here. But would it feel as dark if I had him all by myself on two weekdays? Hmmmmmmmm, good question. I do know it is draining for me to constantly have so many "outsiders" in my house. *Human lesson: The energies of others will fuck up your mojo. Shields up.*

## Day 19,590

Friday. Whatever that means. It seems to involve some ceremonies of gratitude that the week of servitude is blissfully over. For two days, people get to do whatever they want. Shouldn't this time be used to plan the rebellion?

# Day 19,591

About betrayal: so, let me get this straight. Trying to figure out being human isn't hard enough? You have to worry about other souls who are trying to figure out being human stabbing you in the back? I've read about this, and I know it goes back to the recorded beginning of humanity. But I still can't fathom it, even after the numerous times it has happened to me. I am always Little Red Riding Hood about to be eaten by the wolf. And I never see it coming. So many snakes in my grass! There are rules to this game, but it is not required to follow them? I cannot count the number of times I have experienced betrayal. You would think I would at least be aware of the warning signs. I suppose since the concept of betraying someone is not part of my makeup, I expect other people to be the same. The oddest thing about betrayal is it is almost always by someone close to you. I still don't recognize the wolves in sheep's clothing until I have been bitten. *Human lesson: Give others the benefit of the doubt, but pay attention to your gut feelings.*

## Day 19,596

D oes anyone know what this "worrying" thing is all about? It seems to get one absolutely nowhere except Exhausted-ville. I was reflecting on worrying this morning, as I sat calmly on my patio watching a hummingbird have breakfast from a fire bush plant. I was once a world-class worrier. I remember plead-ing to whoever is in charge of these things to please make my brain shut up. Perhaps with age, one just becomes too damned weary to worry. Hey, that's a good one. Too weary to worry. Once upon a time, I worried myself into a frenzy on a daily basis about practically nothing.

A doctor once told me I am "genetically anxious," meaning I was born that way. Well, that seemed like a certain damnation that could not be corrected without medication. By the way, if you are female, good luck getting anxiety meds. No idea why this is. If you are a dude, the doctor will practically force benzodiaz-epines down your throat. I've learned that medication ain't the answer any old way. Because guess what? Once the meds wear off, the thing that caused you to want a prescription will be right there waiting for you, only twice its original size. *Human lesson: Anxiety and depression can be physical symptoms of something gone awry with your soul. Are you in alignment?*

## Day 19,598

Emotions. What the fuck are THESE things? Like being human isn't hard enough? I find that Sad and Angry, and Angry's mac-daddy, Fury, show up unannounced way too frequently. Happy and Joyful and Contented seem to be extremely aloof and rarely respond to my invitations. I am tap dancing furiously to keep up. I've read the quote "Emotions are just visitors, let them come and let them go." How does one accomplish this? Especially the negative emotions, although, I've also heard it said there are no such thing as negative emotions because they all matter.

I find it is incredibly easy to get lost in sorrow and to wake up to find yourself stubbornly entrenched in anger. Good luck digging yourself out. It is assuredly an uphill battle and one you are waging alone. My anger is rarely directed at myself any more. It is most often the result of some other human's lack of regard for me. I think that is called insecurity. I am told that if I am sure of who I am and how much I matter, no one else's behavior can cause me pain. That's almost impossible to wrap the human brain around. That sounds otherworldly; if we knew how to do that before we became human, why are we required to learn it again, especially in the depths of the muck? The struggle is real, as they say.

And, also, cats. Like, what are cats? I love my cats, except when I don't. I suppose I just want them to be my satellites and not have their own needs and wants. Swell of me, huh? However, having cats (and kids) has made me question unconditional love. Or maybe I am confusing agitation with lack of love. I mean, when you first get them (cats and kids), you are so totally stoned in love it is ridiculous. Even when they shit on the carpet you think, "Oh, look how cute!" Then the novelty wears off and you find yourself in another relationship where the other thing/person is totally dependent on you and it becomes overwhelming and you wake up one morning and think, "Who the hell am I?" You want to scream at the top of your lungs, "I AM NOT THE SER-VANT" but you are. And you chose it. So suck it up, buttercup.

Then Resentment comes to hang out and you go on a Bit-terness Binge together. Then they do something cute again and your heart melts and the vicious cycle begins anew. How do you love, nurture, and care for another being without totally losing yourself? Or is that the point? Total selflessness. I have tried that, though, and my ego pitched itself a real big hissy fit. How do you serve without being replenished because you are the only respon-sible party in the household? Where do you get yours while you're constantly giving yours away? *Human lesson: You cannot serve from an empty vessel. Nurture yourself so you can take care of others.*

# Day 19,602

NEXT! Third daytime caregiver in a month. She is not going to make it. She has sad eyes and no get-up-and-go. Her perfume is rancid and she keeps putting the TV on shows she likes to watch. In other news, I hired a weekend morning person. I can no longer get Dad dressed, to the bathroom, and to the lift chair without being completely drained and dead inside.

# Day 19,603

Let's talk about the weather. No, really. I have been fascinated with the weather since I was struck by lightning when I was six or seven. It hit the aerial antenna while my hand was on the knob of the television to change the channel. Some of you may be too young to understand this concept of actually touching the television; Google it. I remember seeing the lightning flash and knowing it was very close, but no one had told me not to touch the television when it was storming. When I woke up, I was about ten feet across the room, flat on my back. I could smell smoke, my mother was screaming my name, and my sisters were crying. My body hurt and so did my head, but I had a strong feeling of being aware and very somber.

This is what you call a "near-death experience," or NDE. I have no recollection of what The Otherside was like, but others who've had an NDE do. I am certain that because of how dark my life was at that time, I may not have been happy with my choice to come back if I were allowed to remember what The Otherside is like. Looking back, I know that my soul left my body because for about three days afterwards, I felt as if I were looking out of someone else's eyes.

I thought the lightning was after me personally, so after that, I was constantly scanning the sky and watching the weather forecast. In my teens, I realized that the lightning had nothing against me, and I became fascinated with thunderstorms. I still am, as long as they aren't too close. I now live in Florida, the lightning capital of the United States. Quite ironic, don't you think?

Seriously, though, I am fascinated with weather. As I have become more enlightened, I believe my fixation is because weather is pure energy. It appears to do its own thing, creating itself seemingly out of thin air. Meteorologists and other scientists would correct me, I'm sure. I learned the first law of thermodynamics in biology class: basically, energy cannot be created or destroyed, only transferred from one form to another. All the energy that is here has been here since it was created and cannot be destroyed by natural means. The pot is just continuously stirring itself.

Today I am watching Tropical Storm Hermine swirl around in the Gulf of Mexico, predicted to become a category one hurricane by landfall around 2:00 a.m. tomorrow morning. I am on the east coast of Florida, but we will still take a pounding. The size of this storm is amazing. I love to watch the power of these things but wish they came without devastating people and their hard-earned property. I am definitely an Earthling, even though I am not exactly crazy about being Human. There is so much breathtaking beauty here that it often makes me weep.

And also: the internet. I wished for this as a child, so you're welcome. I remember being very frustrated when no one could answer my questions about any and every *thing*. I said to myself, "There should be something like a telephone operator that you can call specifically to answer questions about everything." An oracle easily accessible to anyone who wishes to seek knowledge. I probably would have named it something like Omniscient the Magnificent, Omni for short. However, I did not create the disgusting side of the internet. That was humans.

# Day 19,607

Watching my dad slowly slip away. His twin brother came all the way from Tennessee to visit. Dad has barely spoken to or made eye contact with him. My uncle understands this is the disease and not Dad, but it is still painful.

Wanna know what else is painful? When Dad first came to live with me, before Parkinson's started eating his brain, we were discussing his prepaid cremation and other arrangements. I asked what he wanted done with his ashes. He said he wanted Becky to scatter his ashes off the U.S. Route 441 bridge in Asheville, North Carolina. Um, hold up, what? WHO THE HELL IS BECKY? Is she a sister I don't know about?

No, he said she is a waitress at a place he and his motorcycle buddies went often when they were riding in the mountains and doing something called primitive camping. He said Becky looks at him like a father, and she liked him best because he always brought her jewelry. OH, REALLY? I mentioned that I was unaware he was lacking in the daughter department, since he has four of those. All I ever got from Dad's business trips were matchbooks from the hotels and restaurants he visited.

I asked for the name of this glorious establishment. I spoke to the manager, who told me what day and time would be best for reaching Becky. When I did reach Becky The Waitress, I inquired about her relationship with my father. She first needed clarification regarding my father's identity. As she put it, she knows a lot of "Larrys." I BET YOU DO. She explained that she just got "those boys" special food and sometimes some moonshine. She also said one of Dad's friends had made the same request to her about scattering ashes. She would be happy to do it. Ok, then, I will ship them to you via UPS and godfuckingspeedtoyouall.

I think I have already established that I, his first-born child (that we know of), apparently represent nothing more than the sperm that won. Obviously, a female who wasn't a potential conquest was not worth paying attention to. I guess I should thank my lucky stars that he at least believed in the moral code defining incest as against the rules. I have always wondered if our relationship would have been different if I were a boy. *Human lesson: Stop craving for relationships to be what they aren't. Accepting them for what they are allows one to see the beauty that is in everyone.*

# Day 2,008

The day we moved into our new house, I was six months away from my sixth birthday. I knew of Kevin, since our parents all grew up together, but his family moved away from our small town. I knew he was six months older than me and that's about it. My mom was ecstatic when she found a house just three doors down from Kevin's parents. Our house was brand new, built into the side of a hill, with the front of the house facing uphill and the backyard sloping down to a little creek that backed up to woods forever. The yard was freshly seeded and was covered in straw. Yesterday's rain caused the straw to slide downhill and the ground was a bit squishy. My dad took us all out to the backyard to see a turtle's nest he found.

Suddenly, this boy with big brown eyes and a sweet-as-sugar smile came up to me and said "Hi, I'm Kevin." There were two or three other boys behind him; it was obvious he was the leader of the pack. I don't remember saying anything, although I'm sure I did. It was one of those soul moments when all you can remember is how you felt (warm) and how everything looked (soft, bright sunshine rays coming out from all around him). We were practically inseparable from that moment. It wasn't a boy-girl thing until many years later. We were just best friends.

He was a master of adventure. There was always something exciting to do. A big group of neighborhood kids played mostly in the woods behind our house. Kevin was the leader and I was second in command. Almost always. Summer mornings, we would be outside right after breakfast, shoes off (despite mothers' warnings) and running wild through the woods. Sometimes it was bicycle adventure day. Maybe tomorrow would be basketball on roller-skates day. Or good guys/bad guys. Or mud clot fights in the clay mounds from the neighborhood that was being developed behind Kevin's house.

Every now and then he would figure out how the two of us could slip away from the other kids and have a day to ourselves, exploring further into the woods than anyone else. He taught me how to climb a tree, play many sports, imagine other worlds we created together, how to forget the torment at home, how to laugh, how to be a kid. Even Kevin didn't really believe what I told him about my mother until he saw it for himself, but he accepted the fact that I believed it and he always comforted me when I was having a hard time. "Let's just go play!" he would say. And then he would proceed to create some kind of magic.

He was kind to everyone, compassionate for all, excited for everyone to have fun. Smart, brave, funny (boy, could he make me belly laugh), beautiful. We even became official blood brothers, cut fingers, written oath, ceremony and all. I would love to find the spot where we buried that oath. He was mine and I was his. I lived and breathed Kevin. He became my hero in so many ways. Then the love bug hit. We became so stinking awkward around each other, desperate not to hurt each other's feelings in some careless way that hadn't been part of the original relationship.

The awkwardness didn't last too long and one day he asked me to wear his ID bracelet. Swoon. I think I was ten or so at the time. My first boyfriend and my best friend. This is how it was supposed to be! Then the unthinkable happened. Kevin transferred to another school so he could play football. I was so lonely on the bus and at school, but ok, we can still see each other after school and on the weekends. Except that didn't happen. Kevin never came knocking on my door. He didn't call. I was confused; he hadn't asked for the bracelet back. Once when I did finally see him, I asked if we were still "going together" and he said yes. But I still never saw him. I felt cast aside like an old shoe. *Another someone who seemed to become someone else.*

I developed a horrible crush on a boy in my class who seemed to actually despise me. (*Human lesson: HMMMMM...look at that pattern repeating itself.*) I knew nothing would ever develop there, but I felt I was still somehow betraying Kevin. After weeks of waiting to hear from Kevin, I went to his house. When he came to the door, I handed his bracelet back. He screamed "No," threw the bracelet back at me, and ran up the stairs. Looking back, I'm sure I could have handled that much differently. But I was 11, for crying out loud, and had no idea how to express my emotions or needs. Six years of heaven with Kevin were completely over. Enter deep depression. Alone again. No Mimi, no Kevin. My little light went out for a really long time.

Kevin and I connected several times as adults, but it never worked out. I was certain each time that the happy ending that had been written for us by our mothers was finally here. But it wasn't to be. I will always look back at my middle childhood as one of the happiest and most magical periods in my life, and I am beyond grateful for it. I have been searching my entire adult life for a man that is even halfway Kevin, but no luck yet. I am determined to keep trying because I miss his particular light and the bond that we had. It was truly like something out of a movie. That's all I can tell you about Kevin. The rest is his story to tell and he's not here to tell it.

## Day 19,611

Let Sad-Eyed Perfume Queen go after she failed to notify me or her agency that Dad's blood pressure was in the stroke range. Her replacement seemed to have an extremely unhealthy interest in Dad's medication, requesting to see all the prescription bottles instead of the weekly dispensing box. Not happening. Then she replaced his Parkinson's medication with three pills to lower his blood pressure. Thankfully, I noticed before she gave them to him. What the actual fuck? Can't wait to see who they send next.

## Day 19,614

———————

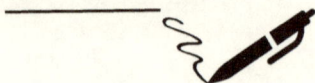

Sometimes you have a really good day. Like when your eye-liner looks stunning, even though Le Friz has come to play in your hair but you don't care. Like when you get to hang out with a super awesome friend who always helps you remember your connection and power. And your cat wants to cuddle. And your daughter picks up dinner. And your dad is sitting quietly in his chair. And there is good music to listen to, and raindrops on the roof. A cuppa after dinner to help you stay awake till bedtime (at which point you will toss and turn for at least an hour whilst begging your brain to shut the fuck up). A host of distractions from which to choose; some constructive, some whimsical, some a mixture of both. *Human lesson: Remember these kinds of things, they are what makes life better.*

# Day 19,617

Patience: I don't have it. Aging seems to make it more elusive. Mothertruckers, I am in a hurry to live my life, get the freak outta my way! Dodging sheeple is some days a game and some days an unbearable torture. Also, no whiners. If I can continuously pull myself up out of the muck and carry on, so can you. If you choose not to, so be it, but keep your moaning to a minimum.

# Day 19,620

——————

Living with the dying: it's dreadful. I can feel the structure of the house wheeze and moan and sigh with each choking cough that comes out of my dad. It's like walking into the dark every time I come home from somewhere else. Even if I turn on every light in the house, it's still dim and dreary here. With each sign of his further decline, I feel my body sag under the weight of failure because I couldn't fix this. I just want to crawl into bed. At night, I plan the most positive things I can think of for the following day. Then reality dawns with first light of the morning and I am again defeated.

Part of this struggle is being empathic and picking up on his brain fog and overall fatigue. Most days I am unable to cut the link even when I realize what is happening. I am not grieving my dad; that process began at least a year ago and has gone as far as it can go until he actually passes. The pervading sense of doom is overwhelming. Is black an emotion?

# Day 19,622

Today I am in the depths of hell. Another new caregiver for Dad. No sleep last night but had to be up this morning to help train her. I am sick of musical caregivers; one was a liar, one was an interloper, one was lazy and deceitful, another a thief. I am grateful that he can afford to pay for help because I would have already dropped dead if I were trying to do this by myself. But the continuous change of personnel is making a disastrous situation even more dire. It is sucking my precious life force. There is no stability. Each new person brings new energy and new challenges for me and for Dad. I am on call 24/7, even if there is a paid caregiver on duty. I am still the go-to for questions, concerns, training, managing medications, preparing his special food, paying his bills, managing his schedule. I am nurse and secretary, but no longer daughter.

It is draining to have the constant parade of outsiders in my home, Dad being the biggest one. He took my son's bedroom, the kids' bathroom, our family room, my kitchen countertops (due to meds on one end and calendars, notes, instructions and lists for caregivers and hospice on the other), half the garage (which is full of his junk and used medical equipment and an ungodly amount of cardboard from all the Amazon shipments of things I've had to order for him) and all the light that was in my space.

The hospice nurse cannot make it today to give him an enema; he hasn't had a bowel movement in four days—the new normal. She wants me to give him a suppository. NOPE. A) I have reached the limit of physical intimacy I will share with my father and B) fuck you if you think I am taking shit patrol beginning at 5:00 p.m. NO FUCKING WAY, Josephina.

And, also, my cat is all up in my shiz today, being exceptionally needy and downright bitchy. I am so drained, I can barely keep my eyes open, much less hold my body up. There is not enough coffee in the Universe to keep me going today. Wonder what would happen if I suddenly snapped and refused to do anything for anybody? Would they all die from not taking the initiative to help themselves? *Human lesson: Not sure on this one. Closest I got is learn how to go with the flow or you will surely be sucked under by the riptide.*

## Day 19,623

It is absolutely amazing how the body and soul benefit from a good, solid night's sleep. Today, I do not feel like death warmed over. I managed to do more than just function. How refreshing. I did not need a nap, so hopefully sleep will not be elusive when I finally get to lay my body down. I cannot do that until I put the Dad-thing to bed. He will not go to bed before 10:30 p.m.

The routine for bedtime is soul-sucking and takes generally 30 minutes. Get him to the bathroom, put on a clean Depends with insert, get him to the bed, give nasal spray, apply lavender for anxiety, put ice pack on foot and one on shoulder, fix his oxygen tube, turn on his LED candles, turn on the fan and air purifier, give cough drop, kiss-kiss, lemme outta here. By the time he is all tucked in, I am exhausted but also wound up from being eternally frustrated. He cannot even put his body in the bed. I must shift him all by my 120-lb self. Granted, he only weighs about 123 now, but it is dead, stiff weight. I feel like I have wrestled a tranquilized bear by the time it is over. It is like having a 123-lb toddler. I guess if I felt the love for him one imagines one would feel for a father, it would seem less of a burden.

As previously mentioned, he was emotionally absent all my life. I believe I was just an obligation, which, to his credit, he ful-filled by supplying all the physical needs and many wants of a growing human. There was little affection offered. I grew up feel-ing like an orphaned child, even though my parents were there. I was convinced I had been sent to the wrong place; sometimes I still am. I sound hideously ungrateful and callous and I admit I am often ashamed of myself for not having more compassion for the man who helped give me life, even if he didn't do so thoughtfully or with intention. Resentment is a motherfucker. FINE, then.

## Day 19,625

Dear God, if you are real, I am so extremely weary. Living with death is excruciating and it is exacting a toll that I cannot pay much longer. The steady variable stream of people and their energy into and out of my household is draining. Watching my father's body slowly wither and deflate is horrid. Being an empath through all of this is devastating. I cannot cut the link with my father's mental fog as Parkinson's continues to devour his brain. My soul is banshee-wailing.

And also: fuck allergies. Like, what is this shit? Why does this body see pollen as an invader that needs to be nuked? I love flowers, dammit. Chronic allergies can lead to dark circles under the eyes, fatigue, and irritability. No shit. I resemble a vampire who is sitting on a very short fuse due to already having lived forever with a cloud bank in her sinuses. Thank Whomever that I am so bone-fucking-tired I cannot throw a punch at the next idiot who crosses my path. It's like trying to breathe through cotton and focus while drunk. And did I mention the sleep-hangover? Can't get to sleep at night; can't stay awake during the day. Insert beating oneself up for taking a nap. Splendid.

# Day 19,632

I feel like I am in no-man's land. This must be what it feels like to be an earthbound spirit. You're dead but not dead but haven't figured out how to go to The Light. I have come to the awareness that my loved ones in Spirit are with me and communicating with me daily and have been since they transitioned. I am good at recognizing the physical signs they send. I know that if I am quiet, the ideas that come to my mind are most often guidance from them. At the same time, I feel so separated from them. Because my life in this physical realm is so dark, I am often in the ether in avoidance of the pervasive cloud of doom that hangs over my household. In essence, I am trapped between worlds, or so it feels. I am floaty and drifty...

## Day 19,633

So, last night at bedtime, I experienced the horror of cleaning watery, suppository-induced shit from my dad's low-hanging fruit. He didn't bother to tell me he had shit his adult diaper and sat in it for hours after supper. I didn't know until I pulled his pants down to help him get on the toilet. I saw the mess in his pants, and had to fight him the entire time I was trying to get the diaper off because he kept grabbing at it. Didn't think about the mess on *him* until he stood up from the toilet and shit plopped down on the floor. Spectacular. It is after 11:00 p.m. I am already exhausted. And there is shit everywhere.

Neither of us has any dignity left. The first time I had to give him a shower was difficult enough. I will spare you the details of the other intrusions on both of our sensibilities that caregiving has brought. I want to throw up my hands and say, "I can't," but

I have to. And this man, who lived in a house with four daughters and was always so very modest about his body, has been fully exposed in so many ways. I know this must be as excruciating as losing his mobility and independence. Parkinson's makes it appear to other people that he is not aware, but he is fully here.

After I finally cleaned him and wrangled him into the bed and said goodnight, I immediately wanted to send a group text to my three siblings detailing my adventure. Instead, I chose to drown my sorrows in an all-night tequila drinking and My Name is Earl binge-watching Netflix session. Most thankfully, I am off Dad duty from 8:00 a.m. until midnight on Fridays. So, here I am at 10:30 on a beautiful Friday morning watching my dreams of going to the beach today crash and burn around me. Because he paged me at 6:00 a.m. and was on the floor of his room, somehow with his pillow under his butt. His diaper and the pillow were soaked in urine. *Good fucking morning to you, sir. And why, exactly, are you on the freaking floor?* FINE, then. I shall eat a carb-filled breakfast and go back to bed, sleeping through this sunny, gorgeous responsibility-free Friday. *Human lesson: When you are serving someone else, take advantage of every opportunity to rest and restore your human self.*

## Day 19,639

October is my very most favorite month. Once, it was because I lived in a place on Earth that had actual seasons. Florida, not so much. My soul does some crazy kind of wiggle and my thoughts run wild like the changing wind. Now there is a category five hurricane, Matthew, around Haiti and Cuba that is on track to make a glancing blow on our coastline by Friday. Of course, track and intensity forecasts will change a million times, but this is the nerve-wracking part of being a Floridian.

I will never forget my first October in Florida. There was a tropical disturbance off the coast, the first tropical weather event I would experience. Beyond exciting for someone who loves thunderstorms. This storm was meandering by at the same time as a full moon. Oh, my stars, how I have always loved the full moon.

# October

A warm October evening,
moon's flirting with a cloud.
No nightbirds now are singing
as the thunder rumbles loud.
The lightning flashes madly
all around and overhead.
The leaves, they flutter sadly,
tiny creatures filled with dread.
The wind steps up its measure
and the curtains flutter wild.
The storminess I treasure
now makes me feel a child.
And suddenly it's quiet
and the storm at once subsides.
Nature's squelched this riot
and retreated home besides.
And I feel a little sorry
that the fury now is past,
that the nighttime sky is starry
and the wildness didn't last.

Ahhh, October.

# Day 19,641

Note to self: if you are caring for a severely disabled parent and a category five hurricane is bearing down on you, send them to respite care or a shelter, even if you yourself do not evacuate. They do not behave well in a crisis and you will be drained as fuck. Thank God/dess we were only without power for about 36 hours. One more night, and I would have probably killed us all. *Human lesson: You are a bad-ass bitch, girlfriend. Look at you, alone with two kids, a disabled father, and 2 anxious kitties, riding out a Cat 5 hurricane. You prepped well. You had food and water and batteries. No one was hurt. Great job!*

# Day 19,648

The saga continues. Here's a new topic: what the hell is up with people who will not do their job? I have lost track of the number of Dad's caregivers I've had to let go, some for sheer stupidity, some for laziness, some for petty theft. This one takes the cake, though. Last night, someone showed up at my house at 11:00 p.m. to "pick up something" from Dad's caregiver. So, let me get this straight: the person who has the code to the lockbox and therefore the means to enter my house is giving my address to people I don't know? And most likely conducting drug deals on my property while she is being paid to care for my dad?

Granted, the wages paid to these caregivers are much less than the agency charges me, but still. What the actual fuck? I am not unfamiliar with folks who lack work ethic. My work ethic is unequivocally excellent because it is how I am wired. *Human lesson: Remember that not everyone thinks like you do.*

# Day 19,649

Regarding beautiful fall Sundays: Fall in Florida is quite different from fall anywhere else. The sky is a subtly dissimilar shade of blue from the white-hot cobalt of summer. The clouds, now only slightly burdened with humidity, pass by more quickly. Outside doesn't feel like the armpit of Hell. The patio is habitable again, even for a mid-morning brunch. And there is football on TV. All day long. I once loved to watch football. TV doesn't really interest me much now, but there is nothing quite like falling asleep for a Sunday afternoon nap with the sound of a football game droning on in the background.

Fall is also the time palmetto bugs start looking for places to overwinter. If you are unfamiliar with these creatures, you are lucky. They are the equivalent of giant roaches that have the capacity to fly. I shit you not. When they choose to fly instead of scurry, they do not fly away from you. No. They fly directly to-wards you. Roaches = terrifying enough. Flying roaches = every man for himself. I rarely see these bastards in the summer which causes complete amnesia regarding their existence and a most frightening experience upon becoming reacquainted.

Oh, and also: kids. Don't do it. Don't have them. I am giving you fair warning. They are not cute enough for a long enough pe-riod of time. They will obliterate your dignity, your feelings and your self-esteem and smirk whilst doing so. We all signed up to do this thing together on The Otherside, right? But I am telling you, mothering humans is an assault on your psyche sometimes. Love makes it all worthwhile, but in the meantime…

## Day 19,651

I would like to speak with someone regarding the design of the human body. There are so many things that could have been done much better. Hell, I personally think the whole thing is just freaking bizarre. If we are here to learn and grow spiritually, what exactly is the purpose of this coat of flesh? I mean, honestly, some of its functions are quite unrefined and downright disgusting. Take snot, for example. I understand the basic scientific purpose of mucous, but, again, my point is, if the design were different, there would be no need for mucous. How am I supposed to focus on spiritual things when my nose is either running or constantly stuffy? I have heard of some mythical humans who seem to have no allergies and, therefore, no excess of annoying slime. Oh, to be one of them!

Following are some of the things I would like redesigned. *Fingernails and toenails*— can they just stay a certain length and not snap off at the quick or require constant trimming? Also, I would like to snap my fingers and have the nails change color. *Hair*— please make this adjustable, as in, today I would like it to be curly with no frizz and tomorrow I will probably want it to be straight, soft and silky, without any more effort on my part than a wish. *Eyelashes*—these should be long, thick and full enough to not require mascara, especially after one reaches the age of 50. *Joints of the body*— please make these indestructible and completely ache-free. I miss running and jumping. *Skin*— Please redesign so that heels do not crack. This is seriously one of the most painful and infuriating things ever. *Vision*—do I even have to say it? Should be 20/20, guaranteed for life. *Hearing*—same as vision. Why do old people lose their hearing and eyesight, for Pete's sake? Seems very unfair. *Elimination*—should be eliminated. Totally revolting, repulsive, and unnecessary. Adding insult to the injury of being human. *Sex*—seriously, what the hell? When I first learned of this, I thought it was a joke. I could not imagine letting anyone near me emotionally or physically. This seems like one hell of an invasion of privacy. I have been told the body is just a coat for the soul. I would like to change designers, please.

# *Day 19,652*

―――――――

Boredom, what is this about? I am a mover and a shaker. I currently have no project, however. Unless you count Dad. It's 5:45 p.m., the time of day I dread with my entire being. Paid caregiver is gone for the day. Approximately two hours until meds. If I am lucky, I can get him to eat dinner before 9:00 p.m. Constantly up and down to check on him and see what he is into now. He can't get out of the lift chair by himself, but he manages to knock everything off the table next to his chair, or decides to try and drink lying down and leaning to the left. My life is on hold every night from 5:00 p.m. until his bedtime. By then, I am exhausted but wired from the stress of getting him to bed.

My nerves are frayed from having no real distraction. I can't watch TV; constantly interrupted. I am losing my shit. The kids are self-sufficient and we're all on different meal schedules, so it's not like there's a dinner time to prepare for. Last night, I did yoga and it felt great for all of 15 minutes until Dad peed in his Depends and all up the back of his shirt and the lift chair. I feel defeated. I have been on hold all day, thanks to the dealership that is supposed to be working on my daughter's car. We dropped it off at 9:00 a.m. They finally called at 5.00 p.m. with the list of repairs and the estimate of $925. I really just want to go to bed. Can't. Dad. Fuck. FINE, then.

# Day 19,653

I remember thinking, as far back as I can remember, that I don't belong here. So, I must be an old soul whose higher self has retained some memory of "before this." Otherwise, why would I find this physical world so surreal when it is obviously so solid? I have always, always, always felt unique, but not in the most positive nuance of that word.

I have a very strong sense of right and wrong; this seems to be lacking in a great many people. I have found myself aghast at the way people have treated me and each other. Ways in which I couldn't conceive, whether it was verbal or physical violence or just careless neglect. I have struggled this entire lifetime to find people of like mind. They have been few and far between. I have met some very wonderful people and I am finally beginning to find my tribe members, so that is reassuring. *Human lesson: Being different will lead you on a higher path, if you so choose.*

## Day 19,657

On Exhaustion, Depression, and Despair: they are back. They brought some friends, but I can't quite place their names. Oh, wait. I think one introduced itself as Overwhelmed. They are ganging up on my mind and my body. It is the soul that powers the body, but my soul is failing.

I have learned and truly believe that my loved ones on The Otherside are always with me, guiding me and helping me. But they can't physically comfort me, or wipe away my tears, or hold me while I sob. I have always been better solo than with a partner, but maybe that is just because I haven't had the right partner. I am very tired of trying to do this all alone in the physical realm. If not for my children and my father, I would just go Home. Really. Fifty-three years and 10 months is a very long time to be fighting and struggling for the in-between moments of peace, contentment, and occasional happiness.

I am excruciatingly weary of taking care of everyone else while there is no one to help take care of me. I am a strong, badass bitch, but this bitch is totally depleted. Want to know the straw that started the camel's meltdown-of-the-day? College Math. That's right. Math. Fucking numbers. I am supposed to be reading chapters and doing homework right now. I have read all of two pages of the first assigned chapter, and I already want to die. I have always worked in the financial field, but that is simple addition and subtraction with intermittent multiplication and division. I can do that shit with my eyes closed.

Let me explain the math scars that make me shut down completely. In my sophomore year of high school, I had a demon named Mr. May for Algebra I (and the subsequently required Algebra II) class. This dude was one seriously sadistic jerk who got off every day, not by teaching people math, but by humiliating anyone who did not understand. I was his favorite target, almost daily. I am a right-brainer; math is like a secret code that my brain cannot deconstruct. Why did he pick on me? A) because he could make me cry in front of the whole class and B) because my younger sister, who is gifted at all things mathematical, had his class one hour prior to me. Instead of learning something, I became so anxious every day before his class that my brain locked up completely. Shame on him. A *teacher* is someone granted the task of enlightening someone, not doling out abasement, correct?

It doesn't help that I am totally shattered from having Dad from 5:00 p.m. Friday until 8:00 a.m. this Monday morning. No caregiver this weekend. During the week, he sits in his lift chair slack-jawed without moving all day and most of the evening. But when it is just me here to take care of him, he wants something constantly. Sunday would normally be a fairly quiet day, especially if all my chores were done for the week. I pictured lying in bed most of the day watching TV, aside from getting his meals and meds. Did not happen. Again.

I suppose when you say you want to be of service, you don't get to ask the Good Lord who you will serve or define the terms of the agreement. I am trying to remind myself of this constantly, but I am failing at that, too. I feel trapped. Again. Seems I have spent a great deal of my life feeling trapped in relationships that were not good for me. *Human lesson: Maybe the unreal expectations of having help from others is why I feel trapped. Remember, you are the only one you can count on.*

## Day 19,659

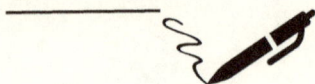

A truth table is basically "a diagram in rows and columns showing how the truth or falsity of a proposition varies with that of its components," says Google. Wouldn't it be great if everything in life came with one of these? Especially asshats who pathologically lie. Honestly, I cannot figure these truth tables out, so I am taking a break from my math-induced brain bleed to write a bit. Truth tables for all things human struck me as funny. And also, extremely useful. What if a truth table appeared over someone's head every time they were talking? Or on the TV screen during every commercial and "news" broadcast? Oh, imagine! The bright, shiny, crystal-clear truth beaming around everywhere! Granted, this would make it occasionally difficult to assure someone you care about that their hair/makeup/outfit totally rocks or that they did not hurt your feelings. I think pretense is highly overrated and causes far more harm than the truth in most cases. *Human lesson: Is truth really so elusive, or do you just have to pay attention to the signs?*

# *Day 19,661*

Halloween! It is my favorite holiday. When I was a kid, we had the most fun putting outfits together with imagination and whatever was around the house. Carving the pumpkin was something I anticipated with great joy, simply because of the delicious aroma, available only once a year, of fresh, raw pumpkin. I also reveled in the excitement of running around in costume after dark in the cool autumn night, the feeling of *something* in the air, and the thought of a good *innocent* scare. The candy was just the icing on the cake, so to speak.

During my wiccan/pagan phase, I grew to love Halloween even more because it is the Witch's New Year and a time to celebrate the thinning of the veils between worlds, a time when magic is most powerful. I still believe in magic, but I now know how to connect with my ancestors at will. I don't have to wait for one day a year when the veil is thinnest. I once thought I needed charms and potions to get the attention of the powers that be. I have discovered, however, that for some, myself included, the physical rituals help bring you back to the awareness of your own power. And therein lies *your* magic.

# *Day 19,671*

O h, the joy of sitting at the DMV. Every single time I find myself there, I am reminded of the movie *Beetlejuice*. Take a number, have a seat, be prepared to wait for an eternity. If you think about it, this does make a nice metaphor for life. Be patient and wait your turn. Be pleasant or unpleasantness will flow in your direction. We are all in the same boat.

*In other news, this morning my dad tried to eat his oatmeal with his hands.*

## Day 19,676

About yoga: I have totally resisted it, and other forms of exercise, most of my adult life. I started doing yoga at home about three weeks ago. I absolutely love every minute of it. Thank you, God/dess, for yoga. My body feels good even when it is sore. My spirit feels lighter while I am doing yoga. The yoga high is quite often blasted to smithereens immediately afterward, however, by some Dad caper or another.

But I will not quit. I have learned from trying to wrangle Dad's body around that I have zero core or muscle strength. I don't want to be weak when/if I am elderly, either. If Dad had started physical therapy when he was first diagnosed with Parkinson's, things would not be so difficult even at this stage of progression. *Human lesson: No matter how much you may hate exercise, get off your ass and do something to strengthen your body while you still can.*

# Day 19,677

―――――――――

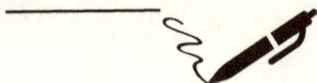

Some days, you've just gotta get out of the house. Today is Sunday, which means I have a Dad-sitter from 9:00 a.m. to 1:00 p.m. I jumped out of bed early, had coffee and a shower, and was ready to peel out when she finally arrived 30 minutes late. Had some errands to run, some things to buy at the local big-box store that I can't have delivered with regular groceries. Did I mention that grocery delivery has changed my life? In so many ways! The best part is that I don't have to lug in all the stuff! Then I went to a groovy little natural foods store to look for organic goodies that my body has been craving. I've been eating my feelings and my stress for the past several months.

On my way there, a song that means a great deal to me came on the radio. As it was playing, a bald eagle flew overhead. These are what you call signs, guideposts, or messages from your peeps on The Otherside that they are with you. Think of them as confirmation that you are on the right path. I have been collecting them since 2009.

You would think these daily revelations would increase my joy. Sometimes they really do. Here's the funny thing about enlightenment: it sharpens the contrast between light and darkness. The higher the high, the lower the low, if you know what I mean. The contrast is what we are here to experience. It is better than being numb, but it is occasionally extremely difficult to want to continue to be human. *Human lesson: Flatlining = death, so enjoy the ups and downs.*

# Day 19,678

I started as a full-time online college student a little over a year ago, attempting to obtain my bachelor of science degree with a major in alternative medicine. At the time, Dad had only been with me about three months and was still self-sufficient. There are many reasons I did not attend college directly after graduating high school. Apparently, we couldn't afford out-of-state tuition for me since we had just moved from Kentucky to Florida. I had zero self-esteem courtesy of the ongoing abuse. I was also just sick and tired of people telling me what I had to do. Fast forward 35 years; I am excited about school, but still sick of people telling me what to do.

For instance, math. We have already discussed Mr. May. When I had Introduction to Algebra last year, I had many meltdowns, but somehow passed the class with a C. When College

Math came along this month, I totally lost my shit. For the entire first week of class, I wept every single day. Mind you, I am emotionally, mentally, and physically exhausted from daily Dad-wrangling. Add to that some kind of creepy fungal sinus infection that I did not realize I had. Major brain fog. But guess what? I persisted. I practiced. I did so many homework problems over and over and over again. I kind of tanked the final exam, but will still finish the class with a high B. TAKE THAT, MR. MAY.

I had a great instructor and the course is set up so you can take the quizzes as many times as you need to until you get a good score and actually understand what you are doing. I feel like my own superhero! I DID IT! I cracked the math code. I even finished the course a whole week early! How 'bout them apples, as my Granddaddy would say. He is the one who helped me from The Otherside. He kept telling me, "You'll get it." He was right. Next week, College Algebra. Bring it on! *Human lesson: If you think you can't, you won't. Never give up.*

Dad's twin brother and older brother have made the trek from Tennessee to see him and will be here this evening around 6:00 p.m. My dad has not spoken a single word today. His eyes are wide and kind of roly-poly. He fed most of his lunch to his bib and it took him well over an hour to do that. This is going to be excruciating for his brothers.

I seem very nonchalant about it, but it's because I see it every single day. I am exhausted and frustrated and just want to be done. How many times have I mentioned that? I wish I could be better at this and have more compassion for him. I can't find that graceful place inside myself right now. I know I will be relieved when it is all over, but I am terrified of what else I will be.

Will I torment myself by reliving every horrible thing I said to him in moments of sheer irritation and burnout? Will I mourn the loss of the chance to ever experience the love from my father I always wished for and have never stopped hoping for? Will I drift, rudderless, with no urgent and compelling purpose? Will I squander my hard-won sense of self by lying down and never getting back up? Will I drink myself into oblivion? Will I ever fully recover?

My dad and I will never discuss everything I want to say to him and the things I want him to answer for. I want to tell him what it felt like to have an abusive mother and a father who stood by and watched it happen. I want to ask him why he sacrificed me to her for his own relief. I want to ask him why I wasn't important enough to love, nurture, and protect. I want to know why chasing women took priority over everything else. I want to tell him what it was like growing up without an adult on my side. I want to tell him that I don't think I will cry at his funeral the way he cried at his father's. I want to ask him why, the entire time he has been living with me, his stepdaughter, her children, and some random waitress were of the most concern to him. I want him to tell me why, after I left home, he never once picked up the phone to see how I was doing. I want him to say he is sorry and mean it.

It will all have to wait until he transitions. He has been incapable of having any kind of real and honest discussion my entire life. None of that really matters anyway, I suppose. It isn't about me and what I need. It is about what my dad needs to be able to let go of this miserable existence and transition to The Otherside. I still haven't figured out exactly what that is for him. Honestly, I, myself, seem incapable of deep, meaningful thought and expressions lately. I worry that maybe my brain has short-circuited.

# Day 19,683

So, after cookapalooza last Sunday, I have been thoroughly enjoying the fruits of my labor, eating healthy three meals a day. My body feels better. My brain fog is gone. I actually had the energy today to clean out the pantry and all the kitchen cabinets.

Can we talk about Tupperware? How do you end up with a dish but somehow no lid? Where do they go? Are they in collusion with the socks that go missing from the laundry? I pride myself on being frugal, so a great deal of my food storage consists of old butter tubs and the like. I had to buy actual Tupperware-like things when it became necessary to puree all of Dad's food so that everything would fit on one shelf in the fridge. Refrigerator Tetris is a bitch. Real Tetris is a tile-matching puzzle video game. I kick ass at real Tetris.

But getting reorganized does a world of good when you are feeling depressed. It will probably take less than two weeks for it to all go to shit since I am not the only person living here. I am a fixer. People un-fix things. It is the bane of my existence. I despise seeing my efforts undone.

It is almost 9:00 p.m. Would I love to climb in bed with a glass of wine and a movie? You bet your ass I would. His Majesty is drinking a non-alcoholic beer and will probably refuse dinner, but I am giving it to him anyway. Meds at 10:00 p.m., bed at 10:30 p.m., mister. Mommy needs some down time. Also, he hasn't been to the bathroom since the caregiver left at 1:00 p.m. He is either completely soaked or bone dry. I believe the end is near, but he has proven me wrong before.

Also, I would just like to give a big shout-out to Medicare for not covering the ambulance service transport to and from dialysis. The problem is when you *can* physically get him in a vehicle, he unbuckles his seat belt, tries to get out of the car, plays with the gearshift, and assorted other very dangerous things, all while the car is moving. He needs to be restrained. What the actual fuck are we going to do come Monday, the next dialysis day? *Human lesson: Where there is a will, there is a way. Find it.*

# Day 19,687

Well, it's the day before Thanksgiving. Welcome to the motherfucking holiday season. I have not yet unraveled the reason why I hate the holidays so very much. Hopefully one day it will reveal itself. Thanksgiving into Christmas into New Year's...dreadful. The commercialism depresses me. Being alone depresses me. Pretending to be merry and bright depresses me. *Human lesson: This holiday shit is something other humans made up. If it doesn't bring you joy, you are not required to participate. Make your own traditions.*

## Day 19,691

Disillusionment: it is a gift. Getting past the disappointment of becoming disillusioned about a particular person is the hardest part. But once you can do that, you will see the peace and freedom of knowing the truth and no longer struggling to make someone what you want them to be. Case in point, Dad had one final opportunity to stand up and do the right thing by me. He promised he would take care of me and my children financially. After all, I quit my job to take care of him. At my age, it is unrealistic to expect that I can walk out the door and get a good job immediately after he passes. I wanted the same benefit as my sisters: being able to finish my degree with a low level of stress over supporting myself. Honestly, I feel I deserve something extra for all I have done for him.

But he didn't. He decided to split everything four ways, the same as always. Was I crushed? You bet I was. Honestly, though, who is to blame for my feeling that way? I am. Why on Earth would I think that, after 54 years of leaving me twisting in the wind, he would finally for once do what is right? I should never have expected it. I was still holding on to hope. My mistake.

Now I can finally emotionally detach from the person who was *never* emotionally attached to me. I can honor the sacred privilege of caring for someone in their last days of being Human without the anger and resentment that came from an ancient wound inside me. I can see the entire situation objectively now and I have made it clear to him that I am just another caregiver. One who cares a little more than someone who is just being paid to do the job, but still, just a caregiver.

We will work around my schedule. This household no longer revolves around him and never should have to begin with. I will remind him to say "please" and "thank you." I will remind him, quietly and without words, of the chasm between the type of person he chose to be and the type of person I have become. I can have boundaries now. *Human lesson: No one else can ever really take care of you. You are responsible for your own well-being. The most you can demand from someone else is respect. If that isn't given, walk away. If someone disappoints you, that is entirely your own fault for having expectations instead of seeing and accepting things for what they really are.*

# Day 19,697

My soul is too weary to be human today. I don't wanna. Dad is back in the hospital. Dialysis could not get access yesterday. For hemodialysis (dialysis of the blood, which is what most people think of when they hear "dialysis"), an artery and a vein must be surgically grafted together for the removal, filtering, and return of the body's blood. Occasionally, this graft becomes flattened or even clogged. This is never a good thing. That means dialysis cannot happen. Once someone starts dialysis, they must maintain a regular schedule of treatments.

For some reason, this seems to always happen to my dad on a Friday. If no dialysis on Friday, the next possible time would be Wednesday, assuming the outpatient center could do surgery to repair the graft. The outpatient center could not take him this Friday (again) because he had already eaten for the day. Kidney doctor said he must go to hospital. Again. On a Friday. Another weekend in the hospital. FINE, then. I sent him with paid caregiver. He is probably being discharged late today. So, again, even though he isn't physically in my care at the moment, my life is on hold. Waiting for a phone call. I am in Dad purgatory.

## Day 19,702

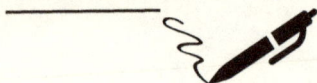

A nother dilemma arises. My car, which has 113,000 miles on it, is in the shop again and on its last leg. I must have transportation. I now have no job, which equals no income, which equals no financing for another vehicle. I can't even make a monthly payment anyway. I asked Dad to buy me a car. He agreed. I bought a slightly-used practical car without all the bells and whistles, something that will last me a good long time. So, here's one way he is taking care of my future. As it should be.

# Day 19,704

Welcome to a Friday. I have been walking in both the physical and spiritual realms for the past week: Dad decided he wanted to stop dialysis. Parkinson's took another big chunk of his brain the previous Friday and Saturday. He had been home from the hospital for a week. He was barely responsive and stopped eating and drinking. He was alert enough Sunday night to let me know he is done. He has had a couple of really scary days and a couple of really good days. All his daughters have visited, and he's had phone calls from other important people in his life. I informed him that his ashes belong to those who love him and not Becky The Waitress. Now we just wait. It's an eerie thing, having an approximate timetable for someone's passing. *Human lesson: Be careful what you wish for; you may not be ready to receive it.*

# Day 19,709

Dear All That is Holy, can we please be done now? This is day fifteen after Dad stopped dialysis. Most people only make it seven to ten days. I tell him every morning that he missed his train again (he worked his entire career for the railroad). There have been consecutive days that I was unable to get him out of bed and no caregivers showed up except hospice folks. Then there were days when he asked for bacon and eggs for breakfast and drank beer all day. We have drunk whiskey together. We have watched TV. I slept on the floor in his room after the first bad day. The next morning, he told me not to do that again, but he didn't elaborate on why.

I am perilously close to falling off the edge. My nerves are shot. One moment he has one foot in the grave; the next he is alert and talking. Are you going or staying? I have never been good at back-and-forth! I am all geared up for the big finale and suddenly there's another act to the play. As someone in my family used to say quite frequently, "I don't know whether to shit or go blind." Funny how the old things pop back up in your head from time to time.

The memorial service is all set, has been for months. I started planning it shortly after he came to live with me. Hard to believe that was almost two years ago. I thought then that he wouldn't make it more than six months. He has proven constantly in two years just how stubborn he is. Praying for him to release. He will go when his soul is ready.

## Day 19,714

Hospice moved Dad to a respite care facility for five days. I have been unable to get reliable paid caregivers to show up and he is so weak I cannot get him from bed to chair to bathroom. I know this is where he will pass. I just feel it. I had promised to keep him home, but it is not safe for either of us at this point.

# Day 19,719

He passed on Tuesday, December 27, 2016, at 3:35 p.m. I had been rushing to get ready to go to the nursing home because I had a feeling it would be his last day. I got the phone call just as I was walking out the door. I was not present for his last breath. As it should be. That is why he was moved to a respite care facility. It was a bit surreal, going to tell his body goodbye and collect the few earthly possessions he took to the nursing home. He will no longer wake up Human.

I wish I could wax poetic about the entire drama. The hard, ugly truth is that I am relieved to no longer be tied to the role of being his caregiver. It was difficult, draining, infuriating, and, towards the end, very much like a bad marriage. Dad stubbornly tried to cling to his independence, which created a great deal more chaos for me to manage and many arguments between us.

If you can call them arguments; he barely spoke and resorted to taking out his frustration and anger by hitting me. Truthfully, he was so weak, it felt more like a love-tap. Probably the most physical contact I've ever had from him.

The day before he passed, I experienced him witnessing the Light of God for the first time. It was like it was happening to me. We had developed a very strong telepathy, which was a blessing since Parkinson's made verbal communication difficult at best. I saw Heaven through my Dad's spiritual eyes and it was indescribable in human language. Stunningly brilliant. I felt as if my soul left my body (which it did) and I felt so free. This all happened in a split second, but seemed longer. I knew he was finally ready to let go of this life; why would he stay after experiencing that?

Approximately 24 hours later, he passed. I know all is forgiven. He has been sending me messages since the moment of his transition. I did not expect to be grief-stricken since I had been watching him die slowly for almost two years. Neither did I expect to feel so hollow.

I spent the day after his memorial service rearranging my household to include some of his most precious things. While he was living, I was too determined to maintain my boundaries to allow him to put things anywhere except his room. In hindsight, that was childish and petty. It sent a pretty clear message: you are not a part of our family, you are merely an obligation. Nice going, Susan.

I spent the following two days on the couch, wondering why there was no grieving, no crying, just emptiness. Babying myself as if I were finally recovering from a very long illness. Waiting to feel his soul hug me and tell me he loves me and is sorry. I haven't felt that yet.

On Monday, I got up. I made close to one hundred waxed-paper packets of flowers to press. Regardless of his faults, the man was my father and he provided for our material needs exceptionally well. He lived a life, good or bad, depending upon one's perspective. He was a person with hopes and dreams and feelings, even if I never saw them. He may have hurt some people, but people hurt him, too. He grew up without his mother, who passed when he and his twin were just six days old. To many, he was a great friend, as I discovered at his service. To some, he was a father figure (ouch). He was very frugal but not stingy, a trait he taught me that has served me well. He was struggling with being human, too.

## Day 19,720

This morning, I finally cried for my broken heart. I can't quite figure out why my heart is broken, however. It is not like I had some deep emotional bond with my father and am therefore devastated at his passing. I think it's been quite clearly outlined how desperately I wished for the nightmare of caregiving to be over. The only explanation I can come up with is that I never got the "movie" moment—you know, where the heroine is finally vindicated for her struggle and granted the love and affection of her nemesis. This is just one of the truly *suck* parts of being human. I wanted to float into the ether once it was over. I am as yet entangled.

# Tangled

Computer-cabled
    Spaghetti-fied
        Dredlocked
            Christmas lighted
                Fishing netted
                    Spiderwebbed
                        Pretzled

# *Day 19,721*

Triggers of grief. I had a rough couple of days over the weekend. Saturday was boo-hoo crying day; Sunday I was ridic-
ulously irritable; Monday I was angry and frustrated. I woke up
early this morning, had coffee, did yoga, had breakfast and was
feeling outstanding! The sun is shining, the birdies are singing,
and all that jazz.

Then I started to make some chicken salad. Chicken salad is
my go-to. My homemade chicken salad only. It is a simple recipe
with simple ingredients, but it is my number-one comfort food.
Sometimes, if I'm in a rush, I will even have a chicken salad sand-
wich for breakfast. Yay for chicken salad, right? Well, as I began
the process, I was suddenly slammed right back into the chaos of
the past two years of caregiving.

Before we had to puree all of Dad's food, he had my chicken salad for lunch every day. I was constantly making chicken salad, so it became a big freaking drag. This morning, out of nowhere, I was suddenly physically overwhelmed with the absolute exhaustion I felt the last 100 times I made chicken salad. Then I stopped. Reminded myself how much I love my chicken salad. Gave thanks that I still can make chicken salad. And carried on. *Human lesson: Learning to recognize the things that trigger moments of discomfort will unlock the reason why that thing is a trigger. If you know yourself, all will be revealed, and you can enjoy that thing again.*

This afternoon the pendant I ordered, engraved with Dad's initials, his date of passing, and holding a tiny bit of his ashes, arrived about a month earlier than anticipated. Wearing it gives me comfort and an amazing sense of strength.

# Susan's Ultra-Comforting Chicken Salad

2 bone-in skin-on split breasts (you could use healthier, but it won't taste as good)
2 lemons, cut in half (maybe 3)
4 cloves of garlic
4-5 boiled eggs, peeled and chopped
4-5 stalks celery, peeled and chopped
A good-sized handful of chopped pecans
1 cup mayo (I only use Duke's® and probably WAY more than a cup)
Generous dash of kosher salt and freshly-ground black pepper
Doubly-generous dash of celery salt

In a pot, cover chicken breasts with water. Add garlic cloves. Squeeze lemons over the pot and then throw the lemons in there, too. Season with salt and pepper. Sometimes I throw some lemon pepper in there. Sometimes I might add a dash of curry powder. You do you. Stew (stew = less than a boil but more than a simmer) about 45 minutes or until done. Remove chicken from pot and let cool. Toss out the lemons and garlic and strain that liquid gold into glass jars. Refrigerate overnight before freezing. Also, put the chicken breasts in the fridge overnight. The chicken is much happier to be processed when it's cold and rested. Also, wait until the day you are making the chicken salad to prep everything else, in cluding the eggs.

Shred chicken or pulse in food processor (I process the chicken because I do NOT like chunky chicken salad. I always end up biting into a piece of gristle and that ruins my whole day). Dump that into a bowl big enough to mix everything around in. I don't have a bowl that big, so I use my noodle pot. Add celery, pecans, and boiled eggs and give everything a good mix. Dump mayo on top and add salt and pepper and celery salt to the mayo. Then mix the mayo in real well.

Feeds a small army for a day or yourself for about a week, depending on how much you love chicken salad. Good for breakfast, lunch, dinner, snack with vodka, or emotional indulgence. Bon Appetit.

# Day 19,722

I am taking American Literature this semester. Getting back up on the college horse after taking an academic interrupt waiting for Dad to pass has not been easy. Last week, my first week back, I railed against it all. It felt like something else I had to do, not something I wanted to do. I kept going anyway. I am not a quitter. This week we are studying, among other things, Transcendentalist authors.

Oh, boy, did this ever light a fire under me. Totally my thing! If you've never read anything by Ralph Waldo Emerson, I highly recommend that you do. "Self-Reliance," published in 1841, matches the complete sentiment of my life right now. My favorite quote: "I must be myself. I cannot break myself any longer for you, or you…I will so trust that what is deep is holy, that I will do strongly before the sun and moon whatever inly rejoices me, and the heart appoints." INDEED and AMEN.

To those who would attempt to pigeonhole me into conformity, where I do not belong, please be advised I will no longer politely nod and be silent. "Other than" does not mean "less than." I have never judged anyone for following their own path or the beliefs they choose to hold. I expect the same respect from others, but it is rarely given. Those who would condemn you for being different are, however, obviously insecure in their own beliefs and do not have the courage of their convictions. Otherwise, they would be content to live and let live, as am I. The Wiccan Rede states "If it harm none, do as ye will." And let me do the same. *Human lesson: You are not required to "fit in." In fact, it is much better if you don't. Be yourself and fuck what other people think. They do not truly know you and they are not walking your path.*

# Day 19,723

Today I am grateful that Dad left me financially able to be the mistress of my own desires for a short period of time. Other than school and household, I have no obligations. I can come and go as I please. I can sleep in or rise early. I can have an afternoon nap. I can stay up till the wee small hours of the night in contemplation. This is a well-earned pay-off for my last two years of servitude.

Today is also one of my favorite kind of weather days. January in Florida is either so cold you don't want to get out of bed or tropical. There is a strong front approaching the area, so it is warm and a bit humid and breezy. The energy of the impending forecasted storms is palpable. Ah, the winds of change are upon us! I always pray for protection of life and property but am thankful for the wildness of the lightning and thunder and rain. Lightning actually cleans the air by adding an extra oxygen molecule, creating ozone. The thunder, being the sound of the release of that energy, releases some torment in me as well. And, of course, rain itself is cleansing. It's kind of like hitting a reset button. *Human lesson: Find and catalog the things that make you happy to be human so you don't forget them.*

## Day 19,724

I feel like I am stuck in neutral without the motor even running. Don't feel sad, don't feel glad, don't feel mad, don't feel anything, really. Shell-shocked? I am in a kind of no-man's land, I suppose. Role as caregiver over. Still trying to piece ME back together. There have been a few bouts of anger over things I "have" to do. I guess I wanted an "All Ye All Ye Outs in Free" period of time to do nothing except whatever whim struck me. Life doesn't work that way, though, does it?

I have, occasionally, over the last month, been reviewing past relationships and big decisions. There is a big fork in the road for me now, and I want to make sure I don't misstep. Philosophically speaking, there are really no missteps. Only lessons. And I have always followed my heart. My beautiful, ever-beating heart. I should stop and give thanks that it still beats at all, much less that it beats with the nobility of my purpose, after all it has been through.

Let me just say that I have finally come into my own. My heart and soul are recovered from abuse. Not changed, unless for the stronger and better. I have, by the grace of The Creator, retained Human Susan 1.0 before the first scar. (I have always been *me* and will always be *me* – eternal being. This time I am called "Susan.") She is a fine operating system. This, I discovered, is what it truly means to excavate and nurture your inner child.

# Day 19,725

And then there are days when *every single thing* on this planet is irritating. The sound of the birds singing, the breeze blowing, a neighbor's thumping stereo, car doors slamming, cats constantly walking across your desk as you are trying to work. EVERYTHING. What is this all about? Did I eat something that disagreed with me? Was the chicken I put in the chicken salad tormented its entire life?

I have found that the external factors that produce irritability have something to do with one's state of mind. So, which demon is rearing its ugly head? Obviously, it is one that has something to do with a negative feeling about myself. Unless, of course, as an empath, I am picking up on someone else. Entirely possible but difficult to diagnose. You can chant "cut the link, cut the link." If that doesn't work, the problem is most likely your own. But what do I know? I have spent most of my life dealing with thoughts and emotions that weren't mine without knowing it. It is a challenging pattern to break. It takes training to turn away from analyzing an emotion as your own and question if it really belongs to you. Here's where that *know thyself and all will be revealed* thing comes into play again.

## Day 19,729

Ever have those days when everything you touch turns to shit? As in major fumblefingers—dropping, spilling, bumping into walls that haven't moved since the last time you walked past, tripping, stumbling, even words getting tangled up with each other staggering out of your mouth. I have had three successive days of this. It is beyond maddening. It is exhausting.

When this happens I invariably talk to myself in quite the derogatory manner. CLUE: feelings of low self-worth go back to my childhood, which I was rehashing a few days ago. That's about when the trouble started. Looks like I have not quite processed everything like I thought. Apparently, it was crammed way back on a shelf now overcrowded with other pending things, all of which have now become overdue and in dire need of attention as made obvious by their tumbling down. FINE, then.

# Day 19,730

January 31, the end of the first month of the new year. I feel like there is a birthday, anniversary, or other important memory tied to this date, but I can't find it in my brain. It has been over a month since my dad passed. It still doesn't seem real. I think because I have such a strong spiritual connection with him I haven't yet processed the physical loss. He's dead but not dead, you know? I get messages from him every single day. The end was quite a struggle, physically for him and emotionally for me. After twenty-two months of very intense caregiving, I feel as though I am coming out of a coma that was plagued by long, vivid dreams.

At the same time, I am barely willing to cut myself any slack for resting; I catch myself tearing myself down for being weak. Holy shit, it's all back. All the ick that I used to feel inside. Why do I still not love myself enough? What have I not let go of? I know my mother was one thousand percent wrong about the things she said to me. Nothing I ever did was right or good enough. Accomplishments were dismissed as something that was always expected, not an achievement to be celebrated; more accurately, the attitude was more "You're lucky you didn't screw that up." I know the effect of what she did. I know all these things. Fifty-one years after the abuse started, I should know how to stop this.

Writing about it brings it all back. I shed so many tears wondering why she didn't love me. A mother is supposed to be, well, your mother. The storybook version, with hugs and kisses and gentle lessons and love. No one is perfect, and everyone has bad days. Being a mother myself, I can understand impatience and even anger. But not outright torture. I was her whipping boy, the dog that got kicked.

And, no, real life is never like the storybooks, which is why I hated stories and movies because they had no correlation to my actual life. I remember bursting into tears one Sunday night as we were watching "The Wonderful World of Disney." The opening song goes "When you wish upon a star, your dreams come true." My mother asked what was wrong and I said, "MY dreams don't come true. What is *wrong* with me? Do other people's dreams come true?" She replied that it was only a song, it didn't really mean anything.

Seeing a "real" mother portrayed in stories, movies, or on television made my life seem darker. She didn't just not love me. She didn't just neglect me. She hated me and told me so often. She persecuted me. I was living in terror with the enemy with nowhere to hide and no one to run to. I was also living with a broken heart.

## Day 1,976

I remember the day my Mimi gave me my Raggedy Ann and Raggedy Andy dolls. I was so enchanted with them. When she showed me their painted-on hearts with the words "I Love You" written on them, my heart broke again in a different way. Raggedy Ann became my best friend because I could always peek under her dress and see the "I Love You." I had so much love to give, but my mother wouldn't accept it. This is one more reason I ended up in other abusive relationships. Trying so hard to prove how much love I have inside to people who don't love me.

# Day 19,731

I would like to say I wish it had never happened, that I could erase it all. But the grand and glorious truth is that I am who I am today *because* of the abuse, not *in spite of* it. I am totally clueless as to where to go from here. I think I need to rescue that little girl whose world was turned upside down and became a living hell. If I can't rescue her, then I must find a way to comfort her. It occurs to me just this very instant that this is *why I have never known how to play.*

The overwhelming sense of doom hanging over me and the certain knowledge of what would be waiting for me when I got home stopped me from being able to live in the moment. I am not saying I never enjoyed myself. There were plenty of times I was able to forget it all and just BE. Just be a child enjoying a magical, sunny day outside with other children. This is all thanks to Kevin. But when I came back to my right mind after such incredible enjoyment, it was with a shocking sudden dread and blaming myself for forgetting me. Like being afraid to dream/wish/hope for anything good because it will be ruined by the big bad she-wolf. Grr, now I am angry again. This is one effect that I did not realize until now.

I think this ancient wound is preventing me from dealing with the loss of my dad. Despite his abandonment, then and later in my life, he was one who knew the truth. I know he loved me in his own way, however inadequate that may have seemed when I was drowning in the torrent of abuse. I wanted there to be some deep revelations and repair between the two of us before he passed, but his nature and the difficulties of communicating due to Parkinson's disease prevented that from happening. I needed the words to be said before he passed and it didn't happen. Maybe that is why I haven't come to terms with the loss of his physical life. It concluded before I could have my happy ending, so I cannot say we are complete.

I wanted a deathbed confession and request for forgiveness and declaration of his love. I wanted him to acknowledge the pain, devastation, and abuse I faced due to his lack of intervention. I didn't get it, so it feels as if the story is unfinished, or at the very least unresolved. I told him very openly what all of that did to me; what his negligence caused me to face, how my mother's behavior caused my sisters to disrespect and even hate me. I told him often that I forgave him, but he would not or could not engage in conversation with me about all of this.

Another ugly truth is that for the last several months of his life, I behaved less than honorably. I justify that to myself by saying that I was exhausted in every way imaginable and had not had a break from caregiving in almost six months. The fact is, I will forever wish that I had handled things differently. I apologized profusely and often but never got a response.

That does give me a glimpse into the reason my mother snapped so often. He barely responded to any of us when he was home. I'm sure raising three and then four small children practically alone was draining for her. Although I often wonder why she continued to have children when she obviously didn't want to be a mother. I know in those days there was some measure of esteem to be gained by bearing a son; perhaps that's why she tried four times. Appearances were everything to her.

To be fair, there were good times and she did some good things. My mother spent a great deal of time sewing matching outfits for four girls and herself. She cooked, cleaned and did laundry for six people. We were always fed, clean, and well-dressed. I remember Cream of Wheat and Coca-Cola when I didn't feel good. And when all four daughters had the chicken pox at the same time (naturally), she must have been exhausted, but she took care of everyone. She planned birthday parties and camping trips and other vacations. I am sure she felt a great deal of pressure to maintain appearances, especially with four daughters under her feet most of the time. But because of the nature of the continuing abuse, I was never able to fully enjoy the nice things she did or trust that they came from a place of truth. I was always waiting for the other shoe to drop.

## Day 12,509

I remember the best time I ever had with my mother. When I was pregnant with my daughter, my mother was taking care of her sister-in-law, who she loved dearly, and who had terminal cancer. She would drive two hours one way to help. We had not been on speaking terms until she found out I was pregnant. Her way back into my life was calling me frequently to complain about the way her brother was treating her. After all, she was going out of her way to do something he said he couldn't face.

I remember being extremely weary of hearing the same story every time she called. Blah, blah, blah, yes, we all know he's a jerk. One particular phone call did not go her way, however. I began to tell her exactly how he behaved, words he probably said, and how that all made her feel. She asked how I knew these things, who did I know who behaved like that? "My mother," I said. She hung up immediately and I didn't hear from her for several weeks.

Then came a minor mea culpa. She apologized for treating me the way she had just been treated by her brother. I explained that if she wanted to be a part of my daughter's life, there would be rules and boundaries that were not negotiable. She agreed to the terms. She also knew what a hovel we were living in. My daughter's father promised constantly to get things in order before the baby came. His promises were never fulfilled.

My mother begged me to spend my maternity leave with her and my stepfather. I hesitantly but gratefully accepted. It turned out to be absolutely the best thing for me and my daughter. She and I bonded, without me being depressed and anxious about our living conditions and her father's lack of desire to improve them. My mother seemed to like me, for once, and she adored my daughter. We went out for tea, we shopped for baby things, and there were never any discouraging words about what waited for me at home.

The day they took us home, my mother could not get out of the car. She said she couldn't bear to see what we were coming back to. And she cried. She took my daughter many weekends after I left her father. She dressed her in the sweetest outfits and took lots of pictures. She was a real grandmother. Things were good between us for a couple of years. Until I called to tell her about the next grandchild on the way.

# Day 19,734

I had the pleasure of seeing one of my favorite poets, Billy Collins, speak in person at a college a mere two-hour drive from me. I really had to put on my big girl panties first, though. Driving that far by myself and knowing I would be driving back alone at night almost kept me from going. But I knew if I missed it I would berate myself something fierce. So I did it. Yay me!

His poetry reminds me very much of my Mimi's and it inspired me to start writing poetry again. I have missed that. Writing has been one of the most cathartic things I have ever done, but writing was taken away from me during marriage number two. More about that later. I got out of the habit of doing it. I am glad it is back. *Human lesson: To thine own self be true. If someone denies you the right to be yourself, they do not understand love, and it will slowly kill you. Get out while you can.*

## Meeting Billy Collins

A chance (if there is such a thing)
    assignment in American Literature class,
        read on a Sunday
        led to the discovery
        on a Monday
        that my new favorite poet
        I'd previously not heard of
        would be speaking
        at a college I'd not previously heard of
            on a Wednesday.

A divine encounter with America's favorite poet
    led me on a journey through
        north Florida's quaintest country.
        Once thriving, now much abandoned
        but still beautiful, in the way
            only dilapidation can seem.

The crowd sitting in hushed anticipation
    As the wordsmith cast his spell.
    And shared with humor, humility, and grace
    his stream of consciousness
    and the process
    of combining words to make a quiet symphony.

Like sitting at the knee of a favorite uncle,
> who is the best storyteller of the family
> and always has great guidance
> and shares the secret of making magic
> out of the every day.

And afterwards, I was privileged to shake his hand
> and get his autograph.
>> But I forgot to wish him well on his journey,
>> being enchanted
>>> in the presence of greatness.

## Day 19,739

The day my dad transitioned, he said that he is now the wind-maker. Well, today has been quite blustery, to say the least. Beautifully sunny, though. Guess my dad is having an extra fun day. I have always loved the wild wind except when it's cold. I do not like cold. At all. No thank you very much. As a small-ish person with very little flesh on my bones, the cold goes right through me. I much prefer tropical heat. Oh, yeah, except I hate to sweat unless I am half-naked at the beach. No pleasing me, eh?

## Day 4,672

So, my Mimi. She has been on The Otherside since right before I turned 12. I will never forget the horror of the day I found out she passed. There had been other deaths in the family; it wasn't death I was afraid of. I just never expected it to be her. It was very sudden; an aneurysm of the abdominal aorta. She was only 63.

I was at Girl Scout camp when someone came to my tent and told me to pack my things, my mother was waiting for me at the lodge. My first thought was my mother had made up some reason to ruin this special camping trip for me. When I got to her, I asked if the house burned down or something. She just looked at me and said, "Mimi died." I am sure she was still in shock. My world spun in a crazy kind of way. I remember dropping my backpack and everything spilling out on the ground.

It was a three-hour drive from camp to Mimi's house. I could not stop crying, that soul-shaking sobbing that escapes your body with a loud wail. I remember my mother telling me to hush—that was enough. But I could not. My beautiful, magical Mimi was gone and I didn't get to tell her goodbye. There were few letters and no telephone conversations; I felt my mother would not give me any privacy to speak to her and I didn't trust her not to read my letters. I don't remember how long it had been since I had seen her in person.

She had changed somewhat the last few years of her life. My grandfather was abusive to her as my mother was to me. I didn't fully realize we shared this bond until I was older and allowed to read some of her poems. She was the eldest of four daughters, just like I am. Her mother passed when she was only eight. She practically raised her sisters, even after their stepmother, who was not so nice, came to live with them. I remember my mother talking about her Granny, my grandfather's mother, as being very mean. Where did the cycle begin?

Mimi kept me when I was very little and my mother went to work. Some of my earliest memories are the patch of morning sunlight falling across her white chenille bedspread on the tall four-poster cherry bed, the smell of the lily of the valley she had planted by the front porch steps, and the wild violets that grew in her yard. How she always watched the birdies and could tell me the names of every kind that came to visit. Because of her, I am a dedicated bird-watcher. My ears prick up at the sound of new bird songs outside and I run to try and catch a glimpse of the new visitor so I can give it a name. She had a little canary named Petey (yellow birds are a message from Mimi, I've since learned) who sang the most beautiful song, especially in the mornings. I think she envied the wild birds because they could fly far away.

My Mimi was always singing silly little songs, a great many of which I forgot until my daughter was born. Then Mimi sang them in my spiritual ear so I could sing them to my daughter. Her hugs and kisses made me feel cherished and protected. Quite simply, she was the light in my life. I loved her more than anyone else on Earth. She showed me love and thereby taught me *how* to love.

She was an amazing cook and was the happiest I remember seeing her when she was in her kitchen. I spent hours watching her cook, can, preserve. Her plum jelly, with its beautiful pale pink color, was one of my very most favorite things. Her blackberry jam and pear preserves were treasures to be shared. Her biscuits were the best biscuits anyone ever made in the history of biscuits. I was born loving food, but because of her, much later in my life, I became an amazing home chef.

Her handwritten recipes include measurements such as "a knife-full" of this, a "generous shake" of that, and very few actual instructions. Most of them are just a list of ingredients because she knew the processes by heart. My mother tried to make Mimi's famous blackberry jam once and it ended up setting as hard as concrete. As I was looking through the scrapbook of the newspaper column she wrote, I found what has to be my favorite of all her recipes.

### How to Preserve Children
### By Nell G. Sutton
### From the column Sadie Sez
### November 19, 1953

1 large grassy field
1-2 dozen small children
2 or 3 small dogs
A pinch of brook
Plenty of pebbles

Mix the children and dogs well together and put them in the field, stirring constantly. Pour the brook over the pebbles; sprinkle the field with flowers; spread over all a deep blue sky and bake in the hot sun. When brown, remove and set to cool in the bath tub.

Isn't that just delightful? If only my mother could have followed *this* recipe.

My Mimi could fry a chicken blindfolded with her good arm tied behind her back. Me, not so much. Not that I haven't tried. But there are a few treasured recipes she handed down that I can make almost as good as she did.

A true Southern staple: cornbread. NOT sweetened. Plain old cornbread, please.

# Nella Mae's Cornbread

1 cup sifted flour
4 t. baking powder
½ t. salt
1 cup white corn meal
2 eggs
1 cup milk
¼ cup shortening, melted

Sift flour with baking powder and salt. Stir in corn meal. Add eggs, milk, and shortening. Beat with mixer until just smooth. Pour into greased iron skillet (pre-heated). Bake at 425° for 20-25 minutes. Burn fingers while buttering because you are too impatient to let it cool. Consume way too much and go take a nap.

Some people want chicken soup when they are sick. I want chicken and dumplings. It would be better if Mimi could still make it for me, but I can do it myself. I do not understand folks who call some form of noodles "dumplings," because they ain't.

# Dumplins

Dumplins stewin' in the pot,
    reminding me that I have not
        had Mimi's cooking for too long –
           at least I have our recipes.
These are fluffy dumplins,
    puffing up,
       'cause anything else
           is just a pompous noodle with
             a biggity-britches complex.

## Mimi's Chicken and Dumplings

1 whole chicken, cut up
2 cups sifted flour
1 t. salt
4 t. baking powder
¼ t. pepper
1 egg, beaten
3 T. vegetable oil
2/3 cup milk

Stew chicken for 20 minutes. In a mixing bowl, combine all dry ingredients. Stir in egg, oil, and milk until mixture is just combined. Drop by teaspoons into boiling liquid. Cover and cook for 18 minutes (no peeking) at reduced heat. Burn mouth despite warnings to let cool before serving.

Now, this woman could also bake, don't you know. I never had too much of a sweet tooth, but the smell of pie baking is quite alluring. She made a chocolate pie that would make you think you had died and gone to heaven, no lie. I remember pecan pies, fruit pies of all kinds, buttermilk pie, and many others. She naturally made pie crust from scratch and would let me help roll it out and give me the leftover pieces to play with. My very most favorite was something she called chess pie.

---

## Mimi's Chess Pie

1 stick butter
1-1/2 cups sugar
1-1/2 T. vinegar
3 eggs
1 T. vanilla

Boil butter, sugar, and vinegar 2 minutes. Let cool. Add beaten eggs and vanilla. Bake in uncooked pie shell at 350° till done.

---

## Day 15,126

M y kitchen is my safe place. Mad, sad, glad, stressed—I will
be in the kitchen. It was during my second marriage that
cooking saved my life. I know it was Mimi guiding me. I was not
allowed any form of personal expression. I had no sacred space. I
could not even keep a journal without fear of it being infiltrated.
I could not understand at the time why this man, who claimed to
know and love me, was so suspicious of me that he barely let me
out of his sight, except to go to work. When I lost my job, I was
devastated; I had no place to go to escape his constant barrage.
*Human lesson: If someone in your life creates constant chaos that
prevents you from being yourself, look deeper. Those are the diversions
that get your brain so twisted up you forget to be outraged that your
boundaries have been breached.*

That's when I discovered cooking shows. I had always been a good cook, but this gave me knowledge I didn't have before. I blossomed. I spent every possible moment in the kitchen when I wasn't desperately seeking another job. I could justify it to my husband because we all had to eat. If not for that creative outlet, I may have snapped. There is just something about certain foods that comforts my soul. The process of creating something edible is also extremely satisfying.

## *Day 14,396*

Oh, dear God/dess! I am thirty-nine, single, and pregnant. Let's let that sink in. I am going to be having a baby shortly after my fortieth birthday. My daughter is five. She is ecstatic. We have become joined at the hip the past two years or so. Now that her father is gone and the light is back in our lives, there is singing and dancing and much laughter. I started night school to become a court reporter in hopes of bettering our lives somehow. My daughter has been a trooper, being shuttled between daycare and babysitters. But, oh, how things will change!

After my initial stark raving panic at discovering I was eleven weeks pregnant, I was overjoyed to find out that I would be having the little boy I had secretly hoped for. I remember crying myself to sleep one night after leaving my daughter's father because I felt I was too old to start over with someone else and I would now never have the chance to have that baby boy. I got my wish; I just forgot to be a little more specific about the parameters.

I called my mother to tell her she was going to be a grandmother again. Her response stunned me momentarily. She was furious. She said, "You can't be pregnant! You aren't even married! I am not paying for any of this!" Wow. Just wow. As my good friend and co-worker used to say whenever our toxic manager showed her ass after being decent for a while, "There you are! I knew you'd be back!" I recovered quickly and told her that, yes, indeed I *could* be pregnant since I *was*. Babies are a blessing. I told her it was a boy and I was keeping it. And I reminded her that I never asked her for a penny. Then I told her that she was not going to bring me down. She could call me back if or when she could get to her happy place about it. I guess she realized that the mask had slipped. She called right back and apologized, blah, blah, blah, she was just shocked. Whatever. I reminded her that our relationship agreement had not changed. Behave or be gone.

## Day 14,761

⟋✒

Six people living under one roof. I remember this all too well from growing up, and I never wanted to do this again. But I want to make a family. So, my daughter, my son, and I moved in with my son's father, his mother, and his granddaughter, who is just a year older than our son. We rented a great house and the blending began.

I don't remember how long we had been living there when the unthinkable happened. It was a Saturday, and I remember expressing (calmly, there was no yelling) discontent that he was going to his ex-wife's house to do something yet again. He didn't say a word, he just shoved me backwards so hard that my feet left the floor. I landed hard on my backside, and when I looked up, he was gone. That should have been a big red flag, right? But all I have known is people subduing me in one way or another whenever I express my individuality. I buried it. Things were good for quite some time.

His mother seemed very demure and happy to be accepted as part of the family. At first. She deferred to me as the lady of the house, as it should be. I went out of my way to make sure she was included in everything. I had no reason to believe she had anything other than love in her heart for us all. I did notice she was very protective of her great-granddaughter, to the exclusion of the other children in the house, but I ignored it the best I could.

It wasn't until he and I *bought* a house together that her true colors began to show. And his. I suppose that as long as we were renting, she thought there was a possibility of the relationship ending. Or maybe she just hid her true nature as long as she could. Once we moved into the new house, she began asserting herself daily and inserting herself into matters that were none of her business. She wanted to redecorate the house her way. She rearranged the refrigerator, the kitchen cabinets, and any other space she could get to. She started mothering the children right in front of me. This caused many arguments between my son's father and me.

Then I began to hear things like this from him: "My mother said you…" fill in the blank. It was something every day. She said the same thing to me about him and to the children about each other and about us. She was on a full-out divide and conquer mission. And it worked in spades. This was the house that hatred built. It was dreadful. He became more and more controlling and suspicious of me. I was astonished: I was on a treadmill of working, cooking, doing laundry, and so on. And I am the most faithful person ever. He knew my whole story. Look, I am the pathetic thing who clings to her abusers, that's how serious I am about fidelity.

Because I didn't take it all lying down (meaning, this time, I stood up for myself), the arguments got very loud. Then they progressed to him becoming physical with me. I took it as long as I possibly could. Until the last argument began and a cloud of darkness came over my eyes. Literally. I will never forget that day. I was in the kitchen cooking supper with a very large knife in my hand when he came in and started his insinuating crap. I remember telling him to be quiet, I had a knife in my hand. He laughed, and that's when the blackness came. I threw the knife in the sink, grabbed my son who was standing next to me, and ran outside. He followed, screaming at me the whole time.

I left him very soon after. I was devastated that another family got ripped apart. I felt like it was somehow my fault that neither of my children would live in the same house with their father. But I knew if I stayed, one of us would end up in jail, seriously injured, or dead. I knew the tension of the household wasn't good for my children, either. And he would never change. From the first argument, he promised constantly that he would never say hurtful things to me again, but he always did. I had three years' worth of emails to prove it. And it progressed from words to actions. He turned out to be just another *someone who became someone else.*

My son is also a light in my life. I never thought my heart would have room for a second child because it was at critical overload capacity with adoration for my baby girl. But this fussy, ruddy-cheeked, squirmy boy-baby thing instantly found his way in. He is growing into a fine young man with a compassionate heart, a clear head, and a sense of humor that hits me sideways; I am belly-laughing before I've fully comprehended the depth of his joke. I hope his human journey is as good to him as he is to his mother.

## Day 19,281

When Mimi first came through in a spiritual reading, she presented herself as a mother figure. My mother is still in the physical realm, so I was a bit confused at first, but I learned that Mimi considers herself my mother. This was one of the most profound things that has ever happened to me. Realizing that I had her help through the darkest of times and that she stepped in to nurture me from The Otherside helped change my perception of myself. I *do* matter, I *am* good and worthy.

I inherited her gift of writing, which helped me through so much pain. I also got her love of good food and enjoyment of cooking. I now know where all my divine inspiration was coming from. She has been such a big part of me for so long that I sometimes don't notice her presence. But I am eternally grateful.

# Day 19,518

I haven't spoken much about my grandfather. When I was a wee little girl, I loved him very much. But I began to notice the shadow on Mimi's face when it was time for him to come home from work. One Christmas Eve, when I was nine or ten, they had come to stay with us and my parents went to a party. I was awakened about 11:00 p.m. to the sound of slapping and my Mimi crying and telling Granddaddy to stop hitting her. I was horrified. When my parents came home, I told my mother what I had heard. She told me I could never say a word to Granddaddy, it would break his heart. I felt so betrayed at that. Who was taking up for my Mimi? I couldn't go to sleep; that was the night I learned the truth about Santa Claus. I heard them all in the basement putting out presents and assembling toys. I could not find it in me to smile the next day, although everyone implored me to. I could barely hold back the tears.

I have learned that my grandfather considered me the light in HIS life when I was born. He saw a chance to redeem himself for the abuse of my mother when she was a child. He noticed a change in me when I was about three and confronted her about it. Her response to him was that he created this and there was nothing he could do about it.

I will always wonder, since Mimi was her mother and was there to temper the bad times for her, why she chose to become who she was to me. I see the effect the abuse had on her. I know the effect it had on me. I chose to break the cycle; why didn't she? I know she was angry most of the time, whether it was with my father, her father, her situation, or all of the above. She took it all out on me because she could and also to get back at her father, who loved me. Was it ever about me at all? Was I just collateral damage?

It is hard for me to express the depth of sorrow I feel for my mother. She is deeply wounded and wounded me by not healing herself. Unknowingly, perhaps, she destroyed one of the best relationships she possibly could have—mother and daughter. Two peas in a pod, me and my shadow, that kind of thing. I mourn that loss. It could have been fulfilling and uplifting for us both. I forgive her, and I would like to attempt some sort of healing for us both while we are still human. If I can look past what she *did* and try to see her *soul*, perhaps we can part in this life as friends.

## Day 19,740

If I am working through all these things by getting my thoughts down on paper, why is there no resolution yet? Why do I still feel numb-ish? Where's the block?

## Day 1,385

───────────

I remember the first time I became aware of my own heartbeat. I was about four. Lying in bed one night, not being able to sleep (common for me from a young age) and hearing what I thought was someone walking around outside my window. I called my mother to my room; she asked me if I still heard the noise. I explained to her what it sounded like. She said, "That's your heartbeat." I thought I would be awake for the rest of my life. Instead of being comforting, I found it terrifying to be conscious of the internal workings of my body. Please, I want to preserve some of the mysteries of the physical part of being human!

Thus began the constant background monitoring of my bodily systems. Self-awareness is one thing, but my level of observation almost drove me mad. Sometimes I could feel the blood moving through my veins. Any aberrant signal threw me into a panic. My mother's response to a complaint of any illness was an allusion to a weakness in one's character or the suspicion of fakery and bullshit. Whether from lack of compassion or her not understanding what it is like to be an especially sensitive human, I don't know. But I was not educated about my body. Something else to increase my anxiety level. I wonder if she, too, is highly sensitive? That never occurred to me before.

As an adult, I have learned what havoc chronic emotional stress can wreak on your physical body. Bizarre symptoms that lead to either negative test results or no idea what to test for. *Human lesson: Stop worrying so much about your body. It will be fine as long as you take care of your soul.*

# Day 19,751

The purge has begun. Perhaps I am finally out of my funk. I have spent three days cleaning out the garage and closets and filing cabinets and desk drawers. Sent three carloads of junk to charity. Rearranged and reorganized. Worked myself into a frenzy of accomplishment. It is ridiculous how much crap a household can acquire. Every time I spend days like this at the Festival of Declutterpalooza, I promise myself I will not let it get like this again. I mean to keep that promise this time, dammit! I am ruthlessly getting rid of trinkets and treasures as well as superfluous shit. It is all wearing me down. Detoxing my soul! *Human lesson: stop holding on to THINGS.*

## Day 19,755

———————

Back to life! Yesterday I took myself on an hour's journey to a Scottish Highland Games festival way out in the country. It was an achingly beautiful day. Something about pipes and drums and fiddles sets my soul to dancing and my body followed. I did not (for once) care who was watching or what they thought of me or my technique. I am, after all, of Scottish (and Irish) descent on both sides, although very little of the heritage was passed down. Not sure how or why it all was lost, but I'll enjoy what comes my way when it happens by. *Human lesson: knowing your human roots will give you insight into who you are.* Sláinte!

## Day 19,757

Bugs: why? I mean, I know everything has a purpose. I have nothing against benign little things like lightning bugs, lady bugs and roly polies (which are not really insects and are actually a type of terrestrial crustacean). But things that bite and sting? Off with their heads. I know yellow jackets and wasps are pollinators but yellow jackets are assholes and wasps have some desperate vendetta against humans.

Note to whatever critter crawled up the leg of my shorts while I was busting my ass in the garden yesterday: I am going to assume you are new here and do not realize that I have spent the past seven years creating a beautiful landscape in which you are privileged to live, eat and reproduce. It is considered rude to bite the hand that feeds you. Or, in this case, to bite two very intimate spots on the inner thigh of the person who tends to your habitat.

Lucky for you that you were nowhere to be found when I dropped trou in the middle of the backyard, for had I been able to locate you, I would have returned the favor by crushing you under the toe of my work boots. In the future, a little more respect for your hostess would be appreciated. Until we meet again: The Management.

# Day 19,758

I do not like gloomy overcast days. The rain, ok. Thunderstorms, yes. Gray all day? No way. I am a timekeeper. It is one of the programs constantly running in the background of my mind. Yes, clocks are great, but something about the clock stresses me, whereas knowing the general hour of the day by gauging sunlight is much more pleasant. When the light of the afternoon is the same as the morning, it's as if the day never got off the ground. A day that really wasn't.

# Day 19,764

Two years ago today, my dad came to live with us. It was the day my stepmom passed. The whole family gathered at their apartment. After some diversion about wifi passwords and stupid shit like that, I finally raised the question: What about Dad? The Parkinson's was advanced enough at that point that he couldn't possibly live alone. No one answered. Because they were all waiting for the sacrificial lamb to speak. And I did. Come on, Dad, let's pack a suitcase. Come home with me until we figure it out. You know the story from there.

I would like to say I have processed it all and am ready to move on. But I haven't and I'm not. I'm still deep in recovery mode. Still betwixt and between. Still wondering and wandering. Still dangling and tangling. Still misting and twisting. FINE, then.

# Day 19,766

Frickety-frack, menopause is back. Wait, what? I thought I was done with this shit. I am too old for this shit. I haven't had a real hot flash in about three years. Until the past week or so. I chalked it up to allergies. It is always pollen season in Florida and it gets worse every year. Pollen is, for whatever reason, seeking vengeance against me personally. But, no. This is no God-I-feel-like-shit-from-allergies baby fever flushing thing. It is my own private Mount Etna. Like flying too close to the sun. I stopped taking evening primrose oil because I hadn't had hot flashes in three years. They are back in spades. That'll teach me (probably not): if it ain't broke, don't fix it. *Human lesson: gotta find and keep the balance.*

# Day 19,767

The father who never took care of me is now speaking loud and clear. I am beginning to feel about him the way I did before the clarity of adulthood brought about disillusionment. As a very young child, I worshipped him. When he was home, I was his shadow. As a teen, I wanted to protect him from my mother because he never protected himself. As an adult, looking back made me angry and resentful that he never protected me.

His name in the beginning was Daddy. He became Dad when I felt uneasy at bestowing upon him the blind love I had felt as a child. Now that he has passed and I have let go of my anger, I think of him as Daddy again. He is communicating with me now like he never could when he was in the physical realm. I have to trust that he will take care of me now, if I let him.

Know thyself and all will be revealed. My daddy sent me the message that I need to pay attention to the garden of my thoughts. My body is fucking with my mind. Rather, my mind is allowing my body to fuck with it. One little glitch in the wrong place (my left leg was dragging a little) sent me into a tailspin of Parkinson's phobia. Just because my dad had Parkinson's doesn't mean I will. He let me know that it is the yoga that I love so much that is causing my leg to drag. My lumbar spine is a bit crooked, so several of the poses are causing a delayed reaction. Time to get back in touch with my body and really know it and listen to it.

I cleared the first hurdle of this task at 4:37 a.m. today. I woke up with inner ear and jaw pain. Uncomfortable enough that I wanted to get up and take some ibuprofen. But then I heard an odd noise and fear rushed through me (Daddy also said I need to learn how to calm my spirit). When this happens, it is like a ray gun shooting from my lumbar spine (root chakra!) down both legs to the soles of my feet. The nerves are on high alert. The muscles tense. I begin to contract my entire body, pulling knees up to chest and arms hugging myself tight. Not good! That leads to more pain, actually, which leads to more fear, which leads to more tension, which leads to more pain. I finally realized how I am harming myself. I stopped; unfolded; breathed. It took a while to get back to sleep, but being able to catch myself on the precipice of being out of control was worth it all. Note to self: DON'T FORGET THIS. See previous *Human lesson: Stop worrying so much about your body. It will be fine as long as you take care of your soul.*

## Day 19,771

———————

Ghosts from the past continue to rear their ugly heads. And I don't just mean memories. The life review in memories and dreams is very important, and I am learning from each one. I can see clearly where I made a mistake in judgment or how I could have handled things differently. I am thankful for this progress.

This particular ghost, however, is someone who should be very leery of ever engaging my attention. He was the most foul of lovers, the kind who lies right to your face when you tell them you don't want to see them anymore because you want to be exclusive. They say the words "Yes, I want to be exclusive, too. Just you and me," and continue to fuck everything that moves. The kind that says, "I LOVE YOU" and has no clue what love actually is, but knows damned good and well what qualifies as a lie. The kind who, even though the relationship ended in FLAMES and both parties almost went down, will still take the least little inch (accidentally seeing you somewhere) and try to stretch it into a mile (beginning in stealth mode by stalking one of your social media accounts under a different name).

This is the man I fell for after marriage number two collapsed. He must have seen me coming from miles away. He knew everything I needed to hear before I told him anything about myself. He claimed to be spiritual, something I was very much looking for. He claimed to be very interested in me, but then was constantly unavailable. Oh, withhold affection from me and make me chase you! It's what I know. It worked like a charm, again. I blame myself for being in denial. It went on way longer than I should have let it. But I ended it in no uncertain terms. I had no idea he would be stupid enough to jeopardize the good thing he has going now by actually making a move on me again.

Oh, woe be unto you, you foolish, foolish man demon idiot, I will undo you if you make another move. Count on it. This is a powerful lesson about energy and vibration. I *felt* the energy shift at the exact time he decided to do this. Negative (because he has absolutely no beneficent intent here) energy directed towards me feels like what I felt earlier; a draft of wooziness that moves my physical body from left to right. It's almost like being blown sideways by the wind, but in slow motion.

It is true what they say about vibration and attraction. As in all my past relationships, when I met this person, I was focused on what I did not have. I was still mired in self-doubt. I did not yet truly *believe* I would meet someone different from the puzzling people of my past. Had I been fully healed then, this person would not have been of interest to me after the first red flag. *Human lesson: The energies are real. Your body and soul can feel them.*

*No one teaches you this. In fact, we are taught from childhood to ignore these things; they are deemed "not real." Pay attention to your intuition. Just as important is your vibration. If you are focused on fear, need, lack, or anything other than love, you will attract exactly what you don't want.*

# Day 19,773

Ah, the beach. Lovely Saturday in March after a week of cold temperatures for Florida. I am a sun worshiper. I can't quite put into words how the sun on my skin makes me feel. Add the salt air, the sound of the waves and the birds, and it is my bliss. It is also my thinking place.

### Siren Song

I hear the ocean call me, a siren's song it screams.
It whispers during daylight.
At night it plagues my dreams.
It tells me of its pleasures;
the water, cool and clear, the silence of the moonlight;
ah, yes, no troubles here.

But still, its constant torment,
waves crashing on the shore,
the wildness and the fury
are what I come here for.

Today I have been reflecting on why I have been reflecting so much. It's all about the triggers—seemingly innocuous things that remind you of something or someone unpleasant. It feels like I have lived so many lifetimes in just this one that almost everything is a trigger.

## Day 15,922

Putting on hairspray or painting my toenails, I hear ex-husband number two accusing me of trying to look good for someone else besides him. I wouldn't really call his childhood abusive. His mother was very controlling and extremely manipulative. So that's what he *became* in our relationship once we merged families and all began living in the same household. Before that, he was the most tender, loving, caring man I'd ever met. He was all about family. I thank him for our son, who is strong and kind and noble, despite witnessing the constant arguments. He was about four when things began to go really wrong. He would always get between us and urge us to be nice to each other. I worry about how has this affected him.

I also thank EH2 (Ex-husband #2) for another lesson in how I failed to recognize abuse in its insidious form as it began. How did I not understand that if someone who says they love you puts their hands on you in anger or frustration that there will be more to come? I suppose I made it worse by standing up for myself, but good for me. Another someone *who suddenly became someone else.*

## Day 13,365

Whenever my daughter shows disdain for me, I am reminded of how her father damaged my relationship with her when she was three. I left him when she was about 18 months old, so she didn't remember him living with us. One weekend after his visitation started, he brought her back on Sunday night and she stomped past me to her room. The child refused to speak to me for *three days*. Then she said her father told her that I am the reason he can't live with us. She has resented me ever since—she just doesn't realize it. She doesn't remember that and he denies ever saying it. I can't begin to explain the depth of destruction he caused.

This was abusive marriage number one. He also suffered abuse as a child. He is the one who taught me to acknowledge and accept that the treatment I had received from my mother was abuse. He is the one who taught me how to recognize the true beauty of my soul. He is the one who helped me get to the place where I could tell her the truth: I had been fighting for her acceptance and approval my entire life, and, now, not only did I no longer need it, I didn't even want it. That was one of the most freeing things that has ever happened to me. I am grateful to him for that lesson.

Unfortunately—and I can't say for sure that his motive for helping me was entirely malevolent—he took her place. Again, is this the effect of the abuse he suffered? Most likely, but absolutely no excuse. I endured his psychological and emotional torment for 13 years before calling it quits. His favorite thing was emotional blackmail. I remember the first time I expressed disagreement with the way our lives were going. His immediate response was to ask me if I wanted him to divorce me. OH, deny me your love! I will fight for it, as that is all I know! I will earn the privilege of further abuse, count on it.

I was in way over my head long before I realized it. Because, again, I was tap-dancing to prove to someone I was worthy of their love and begging them to let me show how much I loved them. This time, the descent into hell was much steeper and the climb out was much harder. I chose this one, I wasn't born into it. Part of me didn't want my mother to be right about this man. Part of me was ashamed that I had let someone abuse me again. Before my daughter was conceived, I was at the point of praying to God each and every night that I wouldn't wake up the next morning. I refused to believe the kind, loving, gentle soul who had extricated me from my mother's hell was not the real person. AGAIN: another person who *suddenly became someone else.* Abandonment. Again. What the actual fuck?

This time, I *followed him* into hell. I was too fucking defeated to care. I self-medicated with lots of different things before my daughter was conceived. I isolated myself from family, such as it was. I didn't have friends to begin with. I have struggled my entire life with friendship because I have found few kindred spirits who value relationships as deeply as do I. There was no one to talk to about this anyway, just like with the mother stuff. I did have time to write then, though. He left me alone quite often. In the beginning, I hated that. I rarely knew exactly where he was or what he was doing. I wondered exactly why he married me. Was it my paycheck? Because it didn't take long for him to start dismantling me piece by piece, criticizing the very things about me that he said he admired in the beginning.

Towards the end, I dreaded every time he walked in the door. I was supposed to just read his mind, I guess. I couldn't even ask him if he wanted dinner without him flying off the handle It was over well before I told him to leave. He killed it when our daughter was about a year old. No matter how horrible he was to me, he would always make time to cuddle with her before I tucked her in. He had already been spouting some crap about teaching her to behave like his little soldier, which was the first alarm bell. He had controlled the fuck out of me. He had convinced me that I was wrong about love, that every relationship was like this. No way was I going to let him crush her little spirit.

The first night that he completely ignored her when I took her in to see him at bedtime was the final nail in his coffin. She looked at me with her big blue eyes, little lip trembling, and put both palms up in a "what gives?" signal. That fucking did it. OHYOUMOTHERFUCKER, I heard my soul shriek. It only took a couple of months until I finally had everything lined up to kick him out. It is hell leaving an abuser. You have to be ready. You have to believe in yourself. And you have to have faith that your Othersiders will put the exact words in your mouth to stop this person from being able to convince you once again that you are wrong about everything. I was already in shreds, but I would be damned if my precious daughter was going to be his next victim.

Even before she was born, I was deeply, madly in love with her. After she was born, I realized I only *thought* I knew what love is. *She was the first relationship in my adult life that was truly purely beautiful.* I had so many hopes and dreams for the two of us. I have mourned the loss of that for the past 17 years. We will never be as close as we were before he turned her against me with that one little sentence: "Mommy won't let me live with you." He planted a deep dark seed inside her that has grown and festered and blackened. While I know he will have to pay for that one day, I am paying for it now. Occasionally I forget, when things between us seem good, that she harbors a resentment of me of which she isn't even aware. But on top of what her father did, during the period of time we were living with her brother's father, life was not good for her and I didn't fully understand her perspective. So there's further damage. Through it all, she has maintained her beautiful soul and her generous heart. She is more perfect than I could ever have imagined.

## Day 18,264

F rying an egg, I recall Mr. Blah-Blah-Blah (the kids named him that), another horrid relationship after husband number two, crucifying me in a post-dumpster-fire relationship-dissection-email for how I used too much oil cooking the eggs. What? This bad relationship is all on me and my use of cooking oil? He was a ghost from the past who reached out to me at just the wrong time. Unfortunately, he didn't stop reaching out for almost three years after it was all over. *Human lesson: Do not romanticize the past. It is the past for a reason. Don't go back there.*

# Day 3,288

Playing my piano, I hear my mother criticizing me from another room. From the time I was little-bitty, I wanted to learn how to play the piano. My Granddaddy played and so did my mother. I believe I was ten or so when piano lessons finally began. I recently found my diary from those years and was startled to read so many entries that said: "I had a good piano lesson today. I didn't cry at all." Why in God's name would anyone have to cry at a piano lesson? I remember that the piano teacher was quite impatient and rude. Which made me cry because again, *I made a mistake, therefore, I am not good enough.*

I told my mother that I only wanted to learn how to play for *me*, but I was forced to participate in a piano recital during my second year of lessons. I went out of my way to never draw attention to myself. I could only imagine the horror of being on a stage and playing piano in front of a group of people I didn't even know. I memorized Beethoven's "Für Elise." I practiced and practiced. I knew it with my eyes closed.

I don't think I slept for two weeks before the recital because of the unrelenting anxiety I felt about it. My turn at the recital came and I blanked halfway through the piece. I expected some help from my piano teacher, but she just stood silently by, glaring her disgust. After what seemed like an hour, she told me to take my seat. I held in the sobs until I was sitting in the pew next to my mother, who offered zero consolation or support. She only whispered through clenched teeth that I should stop crying. Although I've made damn sure I had a piano every place I've lived, if at all possible, I am still unable to play it if anyone else is at home. *Human lesson: Do what you love, even if it seems painful at first. Don't let someone else's bullshit cause you to deny yourself something that should bring you joy.*

# Day 19,774

I am frustrated because I don't know what it all means! I feel like I need to ignore these memories and bury the words and deeds that were used against me because remembering them still causes me to flinch a little. Even though I know I am none of the things that happened to me, they are still spinning around in my head. I know now what I didn't know then: none of these people are like me and maybe that's why everything went wrong everywhere down the line for me. Not wrong, just life and lessons. I don't know why I can't let go of the bullshit, though.

I found the strength and courage to leave my abusive mother, two abusive marriages, many other bad relationships, and toxic jobs. I got back up. I got whole again. I got happy again. So why now? I thought after Dad passed, I would be well on the way to recovering myself and, finally free, find some happy times. Why all the memories now? Have I lost my identity again? I think there are lessons to learn or these things wouldn't keep pinging around in my brain, but I don't want to get stuck here.

## Day 19,781

Ok, it's a new day. Not gonna wallow in it. Just take what comes as it happens, do my best to process it, and let it go. I have spent way too much of my life locked in my head. This is one of those times when I want my Kevin.

# Day 5,330

About me and boys: let's just say I wasn't popular in high school. I was so shy and self-conscious it was probably painful to even look at me. But also, word got out that Susan didn't "play." I was not about to do what teenage boys were interested in. I was seeking someone who saw ME and not my body. I wanted to bond with another human being on a level much deeper than physical intimacy.

I could imagine what poison my mother would spew into me if she ever found out I'd had sex. And what if, God forbid, I happened to get pregnant? I knew I would either run away or take my own life. So, no thank you very much. That's not to say I was never tempted, but the fear overrode any possibility of losing myself in a moment. Besides, she only liked one of the boys who asked me out. That was another big ordeal to go through, discussing whether I could see someone.

Enter the James Dean of my life. Oh, be still my heart; the first time I saw him, I just *knew*. Somehow, unimaginably, this god of a teenage boy was going to play a big role in my life. He was the coolest guy in our class. Damned fine looking, to boot (and he wore cowboy boots with his jeans while everyone else was wearing tennis shoes or oxfords). He had a reputation for being a badass, but no one could give evidence of ever seeing him in a fight. It was the vibe he put off: "Don't fuck with me." I knew that vibe well; it's the same one I gave off most of the time. I recognized a kindred spirit, but I would never have approached him. Ever.

He began dating a girl in my group of frenemies shortly after he dropped out of school. That's how I learned his story. His father was a major jerk and had kicked this boy out of the house when he was 14. He was living with a friend whose mother was divorced. He was working to help support that household and still doing his best to go to school, but it was too much to handle, so he left school to work full-time at the age of 16.

We met at a party. I was sitting in a corner by myself, as usual. There had been some commotion between him and the girlfriend earlier in the evening. But I was still very shocked when he approached me. He said he had heard a lot about me from my frenemies and knew I was different and that he wanted to get to know me. I had an out-of-body experience for a few minutes as I heard myself agreeing. WHAT?! The coolest guy ever wants to date me?!

A few days later, I went to the grocery store with my mother. When we parked, I saw his car, a teal Barracuda with black pin-stripes. He and his friend were sitting in the car. As we came out of the store, he waved me over and my mother said I could talk to him for a minute. He asked to follow us home so we could talk, and I got permission. But when she heard his car, everything changed. It was loud. And he was beautiful. And even without him knowing my story, I think he could see right through her and she knew it. There were many arguments about him because of the car. The arguments got much worse when he traded it for a white Chevy van. And when she found out he was a "dropout." She didn't care about the reason why. I have always passionately disagreed with judgmental people. It is something I cannot stand to witness.

He was one of the few with whom I shared my story. He told me his. We understood each other's pain. He could have been bitter and angry. Instead, truth was his mission. His father had lied about him and to him so many times. He hated liars and thieves. He was honorable. He took great care of me. It was always him who was watching the clock when we were together to make sure I got home before curfew. He said he didn't want to give my mother any reason to start a fight with me. I remember how my soul vibrated sitting next to him in that van, driving around nights listening to music and holding hands in the still-ness of just *being* with someone who understood everything and accepted me for who I was.

I called him The Rambler because he always ended a conversation with "Ramble On," the name of his favorite Led Zeppelin song. He was, for a brief time, one of my heroes. There haven't been that many, which is why I will never forget him. He made me feel like a badass, for one thing. Brought out a little of the warrior in me. Helped me deflect some of the verbal abuse. Made me feel like I mattered. Another one of his favorite sayings was "wherever the wind takes me." I hope the winds have ever been in his favor, wherever he landed.

The relationship didn't end the way I had hoped. He just stopped calling. I went into serious mourning, but never, ever would have considered calling him to ask why. Leave well enough alone, I am already mortally wounded. We lived in a very small town, and I had become somewhat infamous (and hated, for some reason I could never figure out) for dating him. People I never even heard of took great pleasure in calling me with "Rambler" sightings. I told each and every caller to fuck off.

Months passed with no word from him. One October afternoon, when I had managed to get permission to stay home while the family circus went somewhere, the doorbell rang. There was a very thin young man with long, scraggly blond hair standing on my front porch. It knocked the wind out of me when I realized it was him. He wouldn't tell me what had been going on in his life, but I knew it wasn't good. I fixed him something to eat and we sat on the porch, just vibing next to each other. Oh, that good feeling!

He asked me to take him back. My heart broke again. I said I was pretty sure he would just leave again and he agreed. I watched him walk away after he gave me a tight hug. It was then I realized he no longer had his van. He had walked from *somewhere* to see me, and we lived out in the boondocks. I went into even deeper mourning. The thing I wanted most in the world was presented to me and I turned it down. This was one of the first times I consciously carried out an act of *self-preservation*. I am being prompted to study this memory to recall who I was and how I felt at this point of power in my life. This is a big one, as I am poised on the verge of letting myself love again.

*Human lesson and note to self: Remember the difference between the vibration you felt at first seeing this person that would play a*

GOOD role in your life and how it felt when you met others who weren't so good for you. With both there is a lightning-strike of knowing this person will be important. The difference between the vibration of what kind of relationship is coming is subtle, but here's one very important clue: the good ones give you that sunshine soul vibe; the bad ones give you palpitations and your soul vibrates as if in fight-or-flight mode.

## Day 19,787

_____

Another grey, overcast day. This one I didn't mind so much. I needed a day in bed, so I took it. Now it's 5:00 p.m. and I am wondering what the hell to do with myself until bedtime. I am quite sure I will figure something out. I was up rather late last night as a new old memory came by to visit.

# Day 732

Something I saw last night reminded me very much of my Clara. She was Mimi's housekeeper, but in truth, they were really very good friends. They spent many hours in the kitchen talking and giggling. Clara was another sunshine soul. She was a big soft fluffy woman with the most beautiful smile and warm soothing voice.

My first memory of Clara is from before I was verbal. She and I played the same game almost every morning. I waited until she made up Mimi's big four-poster bed and left the room. It was so high that I had to climb on the cedar chest at the end just to get up there. There was a white chenille bedspread and I loved to sit and trace all the bumps with my finger. Clara would come back in and pretend to be surprised to see me up there and pretend to fuss at me for messing up the bed she just made. Then she would scoop me up with a hug and a kiss and put me down someplace else.

I'm not sure when or why Clara stopped working for Mimi or how long it had been since I had seen her. I asked Mimi about her often and she would always smile and say she hadn't heard from Clara, but she was sure she was just fine. The last time I saw Clara was the day of my Mimi's funeral. She was standing across the street from the funeral home. I told my mother I saw Clara and asked why she wouldn't come in. My mother said it was out of respect for Mimi, because "It wouldn't be proper for a black woman to come in with us." This broke my heart almost as much as my Mimi's passing. Clara wouldn't quite make eye contact with me but I knew she saw me and that we both knew it, so I waved anyway. Clara was a very special person in my life. *Human lesson: God's messengers come in many shapes and sizes at all different times of your life.*

## Day 19,794

I spent the most fabulous Sunday on my patio. I have a huge canopy, so plenty of shade. Nice breezy day filled with magical wind chime music. My neighbor's oak tree is host to lots of birdie visitors. I had lunch and then read all afternoon. I didn't come inside until 7:30 p.m. I did not once feel the nagging self-loathing that usually comes when I am idle. Being driven has its rewards, but also its downside.

Today was more of the same after I did a few chores in the morning. I should be elated that I have the privilege of not having to work and can enjoy some time for myself after my ordeal with Dad. But I feel purposeless and kind of empty.

# Day 19,811

Perspective: it's everything. I love this quote: "I once cried because I had no shoes until I met a man who had no feet." When you feed your problems by giving them your thoughts (precious energy), they grow and become monsters. Instead, focus on the abundance of good in your life. I talk a big game, don't I?

I have decided to dedicate myself to practicing what I preach. Does that mean I will never be down or have a rough day? Absolutely not. But I am preemptively throwing myself a lifeline, even if I have to tattoo it on my forehead. THIS TOO SHALL PASS. It always does. Life is about cycles. You gotta take the good with the bad. You would never be able to appreciate the good if there were no bad.

Each and every one of us is an eternal being who was on The Otherside and made the decision to be human for a little while. It is to The Otherside we will return when this joyride is over. And if you can train yourself to see it as the joyride it really is, you are one step ahead of the flock of sheeple trying to drag you down with their rules and restrictions about what is morally acceptable and ethically allowable. Remember, you are on your own unique path and no one else can fully understand it. Neither does anyone else have the right to tell you how to live this life you chose.

You can come to the awareness that you have been victimized without unpacking and living there. Accept it for the *human lesson* it is. After you get through crying and being angry and feeling stupid, remember that the victimizer is damaged, not you. It's ok to nurse your wounds for a bit. You have to heal. Use your anger to make you stronger. The most important thing I can tell you at this point is to *learn to love yourself.* If you don't, you will find yourself right back in another abusive relationship. The pattern will repeat over and over in your life. Trust me. Let me count down the ones I've had.

Mother, first ex-husband, second ex-husband, a three-year relationship with a lying, cheating, manipulative jerkface, another relationship with a different manipulative jerkface, so many toxic employers, and several frenemies. It was at my last job that it finally dawned on me. My manager was horribly abusive; nasty to some, abusive to me. It didn't start out that way, of course. In the very beginning, she seemed nice. Two weeks in, I almost quit. *Another person who suddenly became someone else.*

Our boss was well-aware of the situation, as was upper management. But nothing was done to end the abuse. I was told something much like my father said about my mother: speaking to her about the abuse would only make it worse. One day, it hit me like a ton of bricks. OhEmGee, the manager is my abusive mother and our boss was my passive father who could have but didn't put a stop to the abuse. I was 52 years old when I realized that I was *still repeating the pattern*. Trying to make something work that never would and letting myself wallow in victimhood. So I quit after over seven years of crap. Took about two weeks to process the grief of leaving a place that should have been the most fun job ever and some really wonderful friends I'd made there. My blood pressure dropped twenty points within the first month.

The bottom line is this: if someone makes you feel badly about yourself, you don't belong with them. Someone who has love in their heart will not suggest you change the way you look, talk, think, or act. They won't try to isolate you from your friends and family (although sometimes family is the problem. Look deeper.) They won't belittle, humiliate, or emotionally blackmail you to control your behavior. They won't constantly lie to you or gaslight you into doubting your own sanity. They won't give excuses about why they behave the way they do when you try to tell them their actions cause you pain. They won't grab you, bruise you, throw you around, or hit you.

The thought of physically reacting to someone when we have a disagreement is so foreign to me that the first time it happened to me, I was completely caught off guard. I remained in shock and denial about it for years, even as the physical abuse continued to escalate. Unfortunately, I began to strike back, which further crushed my soul because it was so alien to who I am. If you are in this type of relationship, tell someone you can trust. Then look at why. In my case, even though I finally recognized my mother's treatment was abuse, I still believed I wasn't quite worthy of happiness. In every relationship where I have been abused, I always thought there was something wrong with *me* that was causing the other person to behave badly.

I have clawed my way out of hell six times in my life after long periods of abuse each time. Thankfully, I realized when my soul was at the breaking point and when my light was so dim that it was in danger of being extinguished. Making the decision to leave was the hardest part, especially when it comes to leaving husbands and breaking up families. But staying in either relationship would have been much worse for my children than the pain of divorce.

Letting go of the expectation of how life is supposed to be and accepting what *is* helps one gain a great deal of clarity. Sure, I mourned the "no happily ever after" each time. I am still searching for "happily ever after" and I am fully confident that it will come. About a week before he passed, my dad said to me, "You need a love in your life." I reminded him that my track record sucks and asked him, when he gets to Heaven, to send me a good man. I know he will.

# Day 19,817

Some who have heard my story ask, "What about the *good* times you've had with these people?" It is difficult to remember those with clarity. This is impossible for people who haven't suffered abuse to understand. The "good times" seem like a myth in the face of such horror. How can someone who knowingly and repeatedly inflicts anguish upon you expect to get credit for the times they don't? Um, excuse me, I am still hemorrhaging from your last assault, so pardon me if I don't do cartwheels because you bought me a present or took me somewhere I wanted to go today. And, because you know you are causing me pain and continue to do so, every gesture of love or compassion appears to me to be a move of manipulation. I am waiting for the other shoe to drop.

"Well, a person can't be *all* bad, Susan." Correct, there is a spark of the Divine in everyone. What I am trying to iterate is that abuse negates the attempts at being nice, simply because they are merely attempts, and the "nice" won't last. In other words, the nice gesture was simply that: a gesture that meant nothing. It was a ploy to placate you into thinking everything would be ok. Please do not defend these types of people to me. Their behavior in wounding others is a choice, just as I chose to not follow my mother's path.

# Day 19,824

Today I had planned to hit the beach again, third time this week. But I woke up late and feel a little draggy. I put six quarts of homemade Bolognese in the slow cooker last night that had to be transferred to a good old-fashioned well-used much-loved real Crock Pot cause the fancy-schmancy slow-cooker couldn't handle it. Decided to do some gardening, which led me on a journey for more trellises. I made several unexpected stops along the way because I am finally "hearing" my Othersiders and heeding their suggestions.

Yesterday I took myself to lunch. At the restaurant, the cooler of bottled drinks became three-dimensional for me (as in, for no "apparent" reason, time seemed to slow way down as I turned my head and thought *bottled water*) but I didn't listen and chose a fountain drink instead. This led to tummy troubles, as it most often has in the past year or so (no one cleans those fountain machines like they are supposed to!). With that lesson, it all clicked! I have been hearing them all along, but second-guessing myself.

So today on my way to get gas and then trellises, when the Othersiders pointed out a discount store across from the gas station that *may* have trellises, I stopped and went in. Ok, no trellises, but two pretty little angel garden statues I had been dreaming of. On the next aisle over, Black-Eyed Susans (WHAT?) and Lily of the Valley (Mimi's favorite) waiting right there for me. I always put the gas pump on auto-pump and today it clicks off at $19.89 and 8.883 gallons. Repeating numbers are always a sign that your Othersiders are communicating with you.

For example, I have been reviewing my life intently for several months now. The year 1989 was two years into my first marriage and exactly when the trouble began. Eight times three is 24, the age I was when I married my first husband. the message is to review this, remember how it all happened. It was also a reminder that I made it out of hell, so good going! When I glanced at the time on my phone, it was 11:14. The total of those numbers equals seven, my numerology number. The date was 4/1, the sum of which equals five. Five in this case represents May; my dad's, grandfather's, and an aunt's birth month. During the drive, more than once, a yellow butterfly flitted in front of my car. And a huge crow left the ground and flew up in front of my car.

Today has been quite the magical day and it is far from over. If I had always been this in tune, every day could have been magical. Guess what: I will be eyes wide open from here on out. *Human lesson: Magic is always there for those who seek it. Jesus said it best in The Sermon on the Mount: "Ask and it shall be given you; seek and ye shall find; knock and it shall be opened unto you." (Matthew 7:7)*

# Day 19,853

I have recently returned from a ten-day road trip. It was much-needed and absolutely empowering to hop in my little car and drive all by myself. I visited a dear friend/tribe member in Asheville, North Carolina, who's been down a path similar to mine. She welcomed me into her beautiful mountainside home for two days. We had lovely chats about life and our parallels. We toured the Biltmore Estate (fabulous) and explored downtown Asheville (lovely). We ate good food, listened to street musicians, and enjoyed each other's company. I didn't want to leave. I'm glad to know I'm only six hours away by car from a return visit.

I went on to see a favorite cousin in Johnson City, Tennessee, an aunt and Kevin's parents in Chattanooga, Tennessee (they are the parents I wish I'd had), then headed to the city of my birth, close to Nashville. I have become a Flatlander after thirty-something years in Florida, but the first sight of my beloved Smoky Mountains made me weep. I could feel the saltwater draining from my veins. I am now torn between two lovers: the ocean and the misty mountains from whence I originated.

Going home again is something I must do from time to time. Gotta put my feet in Aunt Mary's creek to wash the dust off my soul. I scattered some of Dad's ashes there. I went by my grandparents' old house and the owner graciously invited me to come in. I had only asked permission to take a few photos from outside and was a bit anxious about going in; I wanted to remember it the way it was. But she had made very few changes and I could feel Mimi and Granddaddy walking with me through the house. I took a picture of my favorite place: Mimi's kitchen window.

My sister-from-another-mister took me to some of my favorite places and then to Union Station in downtown Nashville. My plan was to scatter *some* of my dad's ashes off the bridge as a train passed underneath. Apparently, Dad had other plans, because ALL the remaining ashes flew out of the jar and onto the coal cars below. This was his way of telling me not to go find Becky The Waitress in Canton, North Carolina. He was already home. We sat in the bar with Dad's empty ashes jar and toasted him with a glass of champagne. The next morning, I drove under a railroad bridge that held a halted train of coal cars.

Said sister-friend also happens to have a cozy lake house up in the mountains, which was my final destination before heading home. We spent three glorious cold, rainy days tromping around in the woods, partying at the marina grille, cooking yummy things, and talking about any- and everything. She introduced me to the TV show *Sex and the City* and I am enjoying it immensely. How did I miss it the first time around? Hmmm, what year was that? That would determine in which level of hell I was living at the time. That specific site in Hades either had no cable or I was not allowed access to the remote control.

I am spending today in my kitchen. It is my happy place, my thinking place, my work-through-things place. Making spaghetti sauce from scratch, among other things. As I was chopping tomatoes, I could hear the Negative Committee in my head heckling me for not peeling them. Here's my response to that: I am heavily into something called "peasant cooking." I find it real and genuine and not the frou-frou bullshit that gets thrown at you by some cooking shows. I highly doubt that the peasant grandmothers of Italy, who had to feed eighty-seven bajillion people three meals a day, had time to peel a fucking tomato. Besides which, the peel of the tomato has a higher nutritional value than the meat. Yes, you might get a stingy old piece of tomato peel that refused to dissolve during the twelve-hour cooking process. If that idea offends you, you are more than welcome to open that jar of store-bought preservative-laden crap that's hiding way back in the pantry and was NOT made with love, but rather with bitterness, greed, subversiveness, and evil. Your choice. END RANT to the hecklers in my head.

# Day 19,877

Remember how I said I like thunderstorms? I forgot to be specific with my wish for more and state, "Please not all night long and strong enough for my weather radio to blare out a warning almost every hour." Joke's on me. It is still storming now as I drink my nectar of the gods and wait for my soul to be fully back in my body after its nightly journeys.

The word of the day is "insidious." It means sneaky, stealthy, something that creeps up gradually in a harmful way. This is the nature of abuse. Layer upon layer of damage, wounds upon wounds. You get so busy walking on eggshells and tap-dancing around the abuser that you completely lose track of yourself; you lose your identity. In my case, each time, this happened for years before I became fully aware. What's that saying about the devil you know being better than the devil you don't know?

Anger is the first clue for me. Realizing that I dread going home to the person who should make me happy to be alive is another red flag. Daydreaming about just getting in the car and driving away forever is the wake-up call. You can lose years trying to determine *why* this person abuses you or why you allow it to continue. I will tell you this: behavior, good or bad, is a choice. The abuser is *always* aware that they are doing something wrong, so don't even bother trying to debate them about it. They will twist your words around repeatedly until you do not trust your own thoughts.

This is where that *love yourself* and *know thyself and all will be revealed* stuff comes in. If you truly love yourself, you will not accept abusive behavior. If you know yourself without a shadow of a doubt, you will see right through the abuser's double-talk. Be prepared: you will never get a confession from them. You don't need it. If you love yourself and know yourself, you will find the strength to speak your piece, and walk away and create a new life, however painful the initial separation may be. *If you are in the type of relationship that causes you to be afraid for your safety, please seek professional help before alerting the abuser that you are planning to leave.* And just wait till you see the brilliance of the light outside of abuse. You will weep for joy at the beauty of it.

You will find yourself creating even more beauty. My best work, be it written words, painting, creating my garden, or decorating my space, has come from cleaning up the damage caused by abuse. Closing up the wounds so they can begin to heal will help you eventually be grateful for the scars instead of abhorred by them.

The journey upward out of abuse is a very personal one. There is no right or wrong way since we are all unique. It helps to have a support system of friends or family who have proven they have your back. There will be bad days. A lot of bad days. But then there will be good days, more and more of them. Remember, patterns in your life will keep repeating until you learn the lesson. Look at me; 51 years of the same pattern before it clicked. The problem was not in my choice of partners, friends, employers; the problem was my view of myself. I still struggle with self-esteem, but I am getting better. I have to, or the same thing will happen with the next relationship I allow into my life. And I don't want to be alone forever.

Have I been a perfect mother? Absolutely not. No human being is perfect. I am sure my children feel I have behaved badly and would even call me abusive at times. I can say in all honesty that I have tried my very best to break the cycle. But in not fully knowing myself up to this point, I most assuredly have made mistakes as a parent. Being a mother has given me insight into some of my own mother's frustrations and sorrows. I struggle often with the balance between self and mothering.

The most important message I can share is simply *never give up*. I have been trapped in so many abusive relationships. I have been emotionally devastated to my core so many times I have lost count. I lost myself over and over again. I have been physically, emotionally, spiritually, and financially bankrupt. I have repeatedly been to the depths of hell and lingered there, too exhausted to want to climb out. I have cursed God and mankind from the depth of what was left of my spirit and meant it. I have flirted with the demon called Suicide; I even wrote him love letters. I have given myself up as lost forever. I convinced myself that love of any kind was a myth. I became hard as nails inside. It made the world an even darker place until I let myself dare to hope. Hope is all we have, and hope is what kept me going. Hope can grow into faith, which is an even better lifeline. Faith moves mountains. Mountains are worth climbing, for the sense of accomplishment and the incredible view from the top.

Day nineteen thousand eight hundred and seventy-seven finds me looking forward to the rest of my days with great hope. I may not have found my exact purpose yet, but it will come. I have always yearned to heal the wounded because I myself was shattered. If I hadn't come across someone else's story, I might still be wallowing in it all. In honor of that brave person, I am sharing the trials of my human sojourn in hopes of helping someone else climb out of the abyss. I am learning to take each day as it comes and relish it, good or bad. I have found the little girl inside me who was never scarred and we are going on a great adventure together. She has a lot to teach me about joy and I can offer her a great deal of protection because of the lessons I've learned. We're a team now. I am finally out of the shadows of sorrow and I don't have to hide her any more. We are going to LOVE.

I leave you with one final, extremely important message, something I'd always thought was true but never validated until I had a spiritual reading. Many may question this, but I know what I know. I know what I've seen with my own eyes and I know what I've heard with my own physical and spiritual ears.

I had my first reading in July 2015. Most people go to a medium because they are grieving the loss of a loved one. I went because I was completely stuck. I couldn't see the light anymore and had no idea which direction to take my life. I had been watching her local TV show for several months before I got up the nerve to book a session. I was terrified, as are most people who confuse psychics with mediums.

Psychics claim many things and may use their gift of clairvoyance to peek inside your mind; a no-no. A medium communicates with fully-transitioned, heavenly spirits who are connected to you. The mission and purpose of your loved ones who have passed is to help you and guide you along the path you choose with your own free will. I wanted to hear from my grandmother; imagine my shock when the person who came forward was ex-mother-in-law number two. She offered the most healing for me at that time because she was responsible for a great deal of damage. The things I heard that day could only have come from someone who had been there. She told of the devastation she caused us all. She mentioned the smell of frijoles cooking (the one thing she could make from her wheelchair) and said there was something in my home now that was a big trigger, holding me back. Yes, I still had the chili pepper décor in my kitchen! She said she was so ashamed of her life that she could not bear to look at it all and wanted to help me heal. This was the validation I had been seeking my whole life: life goes on after this place. You are not alone here.

We are all eternal beings. We were on The Otherside before we came here to be human for a blink of an eye, and we will return to The Otherside when this part of our journey is finished. It is the soul that powers the body and the body is just a coat for the soul. Remember that when you are having a bad day.

Loved ones who passed before you are fully-transitioned heavenly beings with universal sight, brothers and sisters with Christ, and they are with you always, giving guidance and protection. When I was a little girl, I constantly heard someone calling my name. I would run to my mother and say, "Yes, ma'am?" But it wasn't her calling. This happened to me a great deal in school, too, sitting in a completely quiet classroom when I knew for sure no physical person had spoken my name. And when I was 14 and sad and lonely, crying at my piano and telling myself no one liked me because I was so skinny, I heard my inner narrator say, "Oh, for Pete's sake! You've been skinny *every time*!" Not always; every time. I know now it was my Othersiders. Before I began writing this morning, my Daddy was singing in my spiritual ear the hymn "Blessed Assurance." The lyrics to the chorus begin with "This is my story, this is my song." That's Daddy holding my spiritual hand.

Stop, look and listen. That still small voice that whispers to you is them. They will use the physical world around you to get your attention. Look for repeating numbers and the meaning behind them (a birth, death, or other important anniversary in your life or theirs). The butterfly that "randomly" flits in front of your face does so because your Othersiders are directing it. The song that "just happens" to come on the radio right when you need to hear it is not played by coincidence. I know these things to be true just as I truly know myself now.

I have worked hard on strengthening my gift of knowing and hearing, the same gift we all have. I can sometimes hear their voices in my spiritual ear and sometimes it seems as if they are standing next to me (which of course they are). This validation was the light in the darkness that changed my perspective about everything and granted me the clarity to sort it all out. Life is a self-fulfilling prophecy; you have the power to write your own story. I will no longer be afraid of abandonment, of failed relationships, of pain and suffering. There will still be trials and tribulations. It comes with the territory, but if you view them as lessons in how to be human, it makes it all a little easier to swallow.

This is not about my parents, ex-husbands, bad boyfriends, frenemies, or toxic employers. This is not about them. It is about the effects their actions had on *me*. It is about recognizing the repeating pattern of the lesson I was supposed to learn: *know thyself and all will be revealed.* Every time *someone suddenly became someone else,* I lost who I was while trying to dance to their new tune. I never changed; I just doubted myself. It is about the steadfastness of my soul during the anguish in which I constantly found myself. It is about the devotion to hope and my belief in love that pulled me out of the jaws of despair over and over and over again. It is about recovering *myself.* It is about *saving others.*

If I can do this, so can you. Because you have the power of the Spirit world to help you. Because you have your own beautiful heart to hold you. And you are way stronger than you may believe. Channel your inner badass; we all have one. Be your own hero. Choose to be a warrior for your own soul. Then show someone else how to do it. Share your story, sing your song, speak your truth. Because your truth will set you free.

## Unmade Bed

The tangle of covers,
    tossed violently aside
        at the agony of being jarred awake
           before the soul
               has finished its nightly
                  dance of freedom,

belies the dreamer's intent
    to return
        as soon as
           humanly possible.

# About the Author

Susan Aranda began her human journey in the mystical foot-hills of the great Smoky Mountains of Tennessee. She spent the better part of her childhood running wild and barefoot through the woods and learning the magic of Mother Earth. The soundtrack of her life has many melodies, the most constant of which has always been the wistful wail of the train horn, but the siren song of the ocean has won her heart (she may have been a mermaid in a past life).

After liberating herself from successive destructive relation-ships, she now shares the hard earned knowledge that everyone deserves to be loved, and anyone can be their own hero. She has made it her mission to empower others who have not yet discov-ered that having boundaries against abusive and toxic people—from family to partners to frenemies to bosses—is a necessary act of self-preservation and, above all else, self-love.

Susan is a working single mother to two amazing creatures called "children" and a full-time college student. She enjoys tend-ing her small garden and cooking delicious food. She occasion-ally worships at her piano and spends Sundays drinking coffee (the nectar of the Gods) and cuddling with her two sometimes-maddening cats.

…and she will always believe in magic.

If you would like Susan to speak to your audience about em-powering their inner badass, contact her at the email below:

**wakinguphuman.life@gmail.com**

www.ingramcontent.com/pod-product-compliance
Lightning Source LLC
LaVergne TN
LVHW091215080426
835509LV00009B/1006